D1418786

Singing Off Key

Singing Off Key

MoVan

Sea Wind
Publishing

SINGING OFF KEY
Copyright © 2006 MoVan
Published by Sea Wind Publishing

All rights reserved. No part of this book may be reproduced (except for inclusion in reviews), disseminated or utilized in any form or by any means, electronic or mechanical, including photocopying, recording, or in any information storage and retrieval system, or the Internet/World Wide Web without written permission from the author or publisher.

For further information, please contact:
Sea Wind Publishing
190 Sea Wind Way, Los Osos, Ca 93402
Movan.com
Ms.Movan@aol. com

Book design:
ARBOR BOOKS, INC.
19 Spear Road, Suite 202
Ramsey, NJ 07446
www.arborbooks.com

Printed in the United States

Library of Congress Control Number: 2005938887
ISBN: 0-9776941-0-0

To Paolo, Kyle, Nico, Cierra, Wil and Elena, for all the joy you've brought to my life and the willingness to sing and dance with your grandma Moni.

Acknowledgements

This book could not have been written without all the people I hold dear in my heart. Some of them have left this world way too early—Mama, Papa, Angeline, Ome Jerry, Ome Nico, Tracie, Richard—but left me with a desire to fight and never give up. By their example I became a warrior in my quest to over come my illness and continue on this journey we call 'life.'

Frances B. Reed, who had her own health struggles to accept and yet continued to sustain me with her humor and words of wisdom when I needed it. There is a sprinkling of 'Fran' throughout these pages.

Shelle, who laid hands on me while performing Reiki, in hope of bringing me back to health. Was it the Reiki, or the laughs we endured during the process of it all? The night you shaved my head, we laughed, we cried, and then we settled for dancing in the living room, holding great glasses of wine. It was the beginning of months of treatments, but we celebrated together.

Bonnie, Pam, Debbie, Marcie, Tony, Karen, David, Bill, Janni, Nancee, Jane, Diane, Zona, Jerry, Douglas—you know who you are—for all the times you drove me to the doctors, stayed with me during chemo, cooked for me, rolled me one so I could eat, and brought out the guitar and sang to me.

My children, as they watched me being rolled into surgery, looking at their faces, knowing I had to fight for them, as I wasn't ready to leave them yet. I had always been their rock, and now they were mine. I loved them so, and as I looked back one more time before the double doors closed I silently thanked God for my children. And now I thank them for always having been so supportive and loving.

My grandchildren, who call me 'Moni.' My first grandson, Paolo, whose light shines wherever he goes. At four years old he translated an Italian song into English for me. He told me I was an old soul with 'a spirit of the young.' How wise he is.

Kyle, who can never get enough 'Moni stories' and is always begging for more. My grandkids in Tennessee who I do not see enough, but we'll always feel the love between us. Cierra, Wil, and Elena, Moni loves you very much and can't wait for you to come and visit again.

My ex-husband, father of my incredible children, do I need to say more. Ex-husband #2 for giving me the 'Van' as in 'Mo Van,' my artist name.

And my husband, what a trooper he is. He met and courted me when I was bald, sweaty, and still sick from radiation and chemo. We laugh, dance, sing (off key) and pray together. We teach each other and are the best of friends. He encouraged me to write this, as he encourages me to everything I want to do.

"Those who say it cannot be done
should not interrupt the person doing it."

—chinese proverb.

MY STORY

From the time I was twelve years old, I have been walking around with the idea of writing a story. And who hasn't? But a young girl **hasn't much** of a tale to tell. So, years later—**having raised** four children, **lain** awake numerous nights wondering how I would make the house payment, **danced and sung** (off key) to many a tune, **designed, (sewn) and sold** dresses to fashionable boutiques, **married** more than once (good friends with the exes and their families), **run** marathons in my forties, **done "splits"** in my fifties, **sold countless numbers** of my paintings worldwide, **faced** a **potentially terminal** illness head-on, and **picked myself up** after falling down, time after time—I knew the opportunity had come, **again** to do something that I didn't really know how to do.

The reason for the story is that I **wanted** to write it. It wasn't necessarily because I wanted it to be read, although I'm glad you're reading it. It gave me pleasure to relive my life, with all its triumphs and foibles, because I did it not knowing how. And

1

the **"not knowing how"** has been the story of my life. I am a happy, fulfilled and contented **woman**! I am a woman who is still busy living life to the fullest **and** one who seeks new challenges everyday. I am a woman who doesn't believe in perpetuating the myth that **somehow** we become less valuable as we get older. "Tragedy arises when you are in the presence of a man who has missed accomplishing his joy," Arthur Miller wrote in 1950.

You are in the presence of a woman who has accomplished and **still is** accomplishing her joy, or just the woman in front of you with 12 items in the 10 items or less check-out line..

I.

The Waiting

The Waiting

Ten days. They said I would have an answer in ten days. How does anyone wait 240 hours for news like that? I lay on my bed in my California beach house, surrounded by my paintings, some of which had been in my gallery, photos of my children and grandchildren, flowers and candles everywhere, and waited. From a CD the Beatles comforted me with their song, "In My Life," as I accompanied them off-key.

If I had owned an old-fashioned clock, I would have heard 14,400 tick-tocks, but now I heard my heart beat. I felt the fear of what I had known might come. I had done everything possible to avoid it, putting in thousands of miles running, eating healthy foods, eating lots of garlic, and working at living joyously most of the time, but now I had heard the word—cancer. It was almost Thanksgiving Day. Did this word mean I would not be celebrating that day next year? I thought of my dear parents, my sister and uncles who had received the same news. They had all died within a year of being told. They had been afraid but never admitted it. I had seen it in their faces. I had asked Mama if she were afraid, and she had only answered softly, "Of what?"

I asked her in Dutch, "Mama, do you love me? Why do you always seem so mad at me?" I wanted to hear her say the words. She just looked at me and asked, "Why do you ask such stupid questions?" We were sitting in her car, in front of her house, with the brick front porch, which my father had built, rose bushes blooming along the driveway, me in the driver's seat. "Of course I love you, your father loves you, and don't ever forget it." I remembered that conversation with my mother after she had been diagnosed with a brain tumor, and myself looking at her, frail, thin and scared. It was hard asking her what I should have known all along. I threw my head in her lap and started crying. I wasn't ready for her to leave me. There was so much to say.

Waiting for the news, I hoped that my children had no doubt how much I loved all of them. I hoped they knew there wasn't anything more they could say, it had all been said. But, lying there, I knew I wasn't ready for the next journey, yet. I was going to be different from all those who had departed before me.

She patted my hand, "Your father and I thought you were funny, that's all." But the fear, she would never admit. I was admitting it to myself now. I was terrified. I didn't want to die. Tears streamed down my face for all those who had passed before me. I clasped my arms across my breasts and prayed. Then I felt a calm.

If I have to, I can do this. Look, Monica, I said, you didn't know how to raise children when you married at eighteen, a naïve girl, yet you raised four beautiful adults whom you welcome as friends. You knew nothing of marriage, you were a good wife twice, and someday, when you meet the right person, you'll be an excellent wife. Someday. I saw a shirt on the table I had sewn for my grandson. OK, as a young mother I had bought a second-hand sewing machine and taught myself to sew. From that I

expanded into selling clothes in the most fashionable boutiques on Ventura Boulevard. I had never studied dance yet,
in a school dance class, I had improvised and created
motions to "West Side Story" that left the class applauding.
And most enjoyably, I had found painting. I knew nothing
about painting before, but I just did it and discovered I had
a unique style. Not only was I selling the art in my own
gallery but in many others around the country. Yes, I had
just gone ahead and done it, throughout my life. With faith,
dance, and song as my tools, I had realized, if you believe
you can do something, you can. There is a saying, "If you
can walk, you can dance. If you can talk, you can sing."

So, however this turned out, I could handle it. I had my
family and, with some courage, I'd be all right. As I lay
there, I wiped my tears and gave a half-smile. I trusted in
God, that God had a reason for choosing me for this. I was
glad he had not chosen my children. I had to be strong for
them. I didn't know how to do cancer, but if that were the
diagnosis, I could do it. And even if I had cancer, I would
go home again, one more time, as those before me had been
unable to do. If I had to, I would **go** through whatever treatments the doctors handed out and **survive**.

Actually, I had seen this future in a dream. I was sleeping one night in my silk nightgown, and in my dream I saw
a hand go from my armpit to my hipbone, and keep brush-
ing against the outer part of my breast. I woke up startled.
It was as if someone were in the room. It wasn't invasive or
anything, just stroking the breast. I had told my daughter
about the dream, and a couple of days later I painted the
breast with paint left over from my pallet; a big beautiful

breast, a big beautiful breast on a large canvas. All the paintings in the gallery were of villages in France, landscapes and local scenes; the abstract painting of the breast seemed out of place. My daughter begged me not to put it out on display, and soon I painted over it. It was exactly where the hand was stroking in that dream that my tumor appeared, on the outer side of my right breast. Had I been preparing for the news?

My life was passing before me, all until now rushing by. I looked up to a painting I had done of Holland. I wanted to go back one more time, to go back for my parents and family, to see our home and the woods where I ran. Looking in the painting, I was back. I was that little girl running home from school in Castricum . . .tick tock, tick tock.

Unbridled Joy

J oyfulness has always been within me. When I was a child in Holland, songs from the radio would set my feet in motion, and my voice singing, as my dark blond hair flew across my green eyes when I spun around. My mother couldn't understand unbridled joy, so she tried to smother it, admonishing me to "act normal." Perhaps she felt she was preparing me for the life of a woman, as she lived it, a life of stifled feelings and disappointment. This wasn't ever to be me. If normal meant to sit still, I wanted no part of it. I would escape to the woods where I could run freely, and there I'd lie on my back, eyes closed, and dream of tomorrows. Actually, though life has challenged me, it is turning out better than that little girl on the soft grass and fallen leaves ever dreamed.

Sometimes I would go to the forest with my girlfriend, Loes, to pick berries. Only the tall trees heard our secret discussions of boys. Our favorite topic was Peter, who soon joined our walks. When I wasn't supposed to be looking, I saw him kissing her, wild berries forgotten. We were nearing the edge of childhood. For me, it was in the warmth I felt when my neighbor's son, Joop, let me walk to the store with him, and sometimes my hand would **brush his coat. Father** had other plans. He had his eyes on a vision of America, spurred on by tales of Uncle Jerry who, at sixteen years old, had first traveled there as a ship's stowaway.

Unwanted News

The news must have been planned, but it came as a shock to me. I was running home from Catholic school one day, as usual, trying to outrun a car in the distance. Running faster would be good luck but, this day, the car overtook me. Worse, I stepped on a sidewalk crack. I was sure the fates had something in store, and they did. That night over a dinner of meatballs, spinach, and potatoes, my father stunned me with his announcement, "Wy gaan naar Amerika (We're going to America)." By the smile on my mother's face, I knew she was part of that secret. My older sisters, Marian and Angeline, were even more enthusiastic, as they envisioned a Hollywood filled with movie stars. I felt sick and excited at the same time.

With the announcement came the required Saturday-afternoon English lessons. Angeline and I would now spend our free time memorizing words from an English/Dutch wordbook. Marian already studied English in school. I didn't mind studying some English, but I had no interest in leaving Holland, my friend Joop, my woods, nor my beach.

Our row house was just right. It was in the village of Castricum, on the street *Koninging Juliana Str.* 10, named after the queen. It had a swing in the attic, two bedrooms and a tiny room with a balcony that I was sometimes allowed to sleep in when there weren't summer guests (*pensioeners*). White lace curtains partially covered the windows, looking out onto a small garden in front, bordered by hydrangea hedges.

Shadows of War

B esides the swing, the attic also held boxes of staples—sugar, coffee, soap, toothbrushes—grownups never knew when another war might break out. I was born in 1949 after the war, but for adults who had endured it, memories were always inside, escaping into conversations when least expected.

I saw few outward signs of the war except for a gray cement bunker on the beach where the German soldiers once hid. Exploring it felt eerie to my friends and me. The biggest damage, of course, was to families who lost loved ones.

War always leaves emptiness—days missed that could have been spent in art, music, love, friendships and inner joy—and lives lost. Since the beginning of time, there have been conflicts, and there will be more, until we all become color blind and blind in our faith, respect each other for diversities, and know there is a God who loves us all. Growing up hearing of war, I felt this. We didn't have a television to see news of the world, but my world had the news of grownups talking. My world in the early sixties in Holland was a safe, happy place, and I wanted to stay there.

We didn't have a television, but most of my friends didn't either. Once a year, however, my family went to the Wouters' house to see St. Nick arrive in Amsterdam by steamship on their television. We also didn't have a car, but once in a while we had a rare ride in one when our Tante (Aunt) Rita and Ome (Uncle) Lou drove to visit from Amsterdam. My sisters and I waited at the corner, cheering them as they approached, and were treated to a ride in the back seat from there to our home. Ome Lou was Jewish and Tante Rita's family had helped him hide during the war.

Canal in Amsterdam

Light over Darkness

The atmosphere in our home was soured by my father's strictness and the need for exaggerated cleanliness by my mother. These clouds would travel with us. This was part of the roles they or society had assigned them; this was how they showed love, but I wouldn't let it strangle me. I secretly vowed that when I had children, "Don't make a mess" would not be our mantra. I would have a house with sunlight, where the delight of living would be more important than strict neatness, and I did.

Years later, Father admitted he could have been a better parent, but that's the way he was then. Laying bricks was something he could understand—hard work, but with everything in order. Raising children he understood less. He probably would have liked to set us in chairs, in nice, neat, quiet rows like the bricks. This was typical in those days, parents wanting their children to be *seen,* but not heard.

My father's corrosive short temper affected my mother. When he was at work, she bloomed like a flower. I could see the differences between sunny days, when he rode his bike to take the train to a job site, and rainy days, when he was at home all day, and we were walking on eggshells. Once, when I was five, my father traveled all the way to New Guinea for over a year for a contractor's job. One day I came home from school, and my father was gone. My mother

13

seemed to relax, to come alive. But when he returned, she was back to her old "normal" self, though she was soon pregnant with my brother, Bob.

These were the people with whom I boarded the VW bus to leave for the dock at Rotterdam: my strict father, my staid, neat mother, two sisters ready to glimpse movie stars, and my little brother. The night before our departure, we had all prayed the rosary at my oma's (grandma's) house, as extra insurance guaranteeing a safe crossing to the " land of opportunity." As I closed my eyes and repeated fifty Hail Marys, my intentions differed from the rest of those kneeling with heads bent and beads between their fingers. As the Hail Marys kept repeating, I kept asking at the end of each prayer for God to intervene and perform a quick miracle. Neighbors came to hug us good-bye and take a last photo in front of the bus. Others waved as we boarded. I felt a rock in my stomach. I wanted someone to say there had been a mistake, for us to get out of the bus, that the trip was canceled. This was my world.

That did not happen. We waved back and rode to Rotterdam. I looked around the bus. Sometimes I felt I wasn't even a part of this family. Even though it had not been my choice to move away from all that I had ever known, the long ride in a car brought exhilaration and a smile to a saddened heart. "Don't think you're someone special," my mother told me more than once. I knew a joy they seemed to miss. That day when I was there with them waiting for the ship, my eyes were looking for what delights America might hold, but my heart was still in Holland.

II.

Coming to America

'The family waving goodbye before the big atlantic crossing. (from left to right, Pap, Angeline, Mama, Marjan, Me, and my little brother, Rob)

The family on board the Ryndam, practicing emergency procedures.

Tossing Across the Ocean

The ship, the Ryndam, a large ocean liner, was impressive from the docks. However, once we were actually in the tiny cabin that held six bunk beds and little else and were tossed by ocean storms, its remarkable exterior was forgotten. All we could think of was getting to the deck to throw up. It was scary seeing so many people in life preservers, hanging over the rails looking green and seeing the vicious waves below.

Sometimes, there was calm, and we could enjoy the food. I tasted fresh-squeezed orange juice for the first time—delicious. A friend I met, Gerda, and I would walk the deck, proudly practicing our words of English, "How do you do?"

"I'm fine, thank you, and you?"

"Fine, thank you." We were certainly going to be all right in America. We were ready when, ten days later, everyone started talking about the Statue of Liberty. "Look, over there."

"Can't you see her? She's a beautiful bluish-green lady with a torch." For some it meant freedom, for others, just a chance to be on solid ground and able to hold down a meal. For all it meant facing the U.S. Immigration official at Ellis Island.

A Warm Welcome

I n long lines, holding our belongings, we advanced toward the guards, everyone hoping to pass the health check and answer any questions correctly.

As a child, I hoped my parents had all the answers. My eyes were darting around the large immigration station room. I saw a friendly worker helping people with their boxes and bags. He was Black. The only person I had seen with that dark skin color was our doctor in Castricum, so he must also be a doctor. I smiled. His face lit up, and he returned the gesture. Then he spoke to my mother and father. "She is special, look at that smile," he declared. I beamed. After so long of being told I was *not* special, here was someone confirming that I *was.* I knew what the word meant because it is so close to the Dutch word, *speciaal.* I now felt welcome in this new country, though I still would have preferred to be in Holland.

After inspections, I bade good-bye to Gerda, hoping we'd see each other again, but knowing we wouldn't, except in memories, and we went to dock in Hoboken.

There we learned we were not to travel by train, but by plane, off to Burbank, California. This was certainly easier than the ship and was another new experience. In Burbank, my father, without English, tried to convey directions to the cab driver. Result: It took us three hours to find my uncle's house in Panorama City, only thirty miles away. I was determined that I would learn this new language as soon as possible.

Work Begins

Though I was soon in school, I was just as soon at work. Days of picking berries in the forest and being in a school where I understood the teacher were replaced. Now, by day I was hearing a teacher whose words had no meaning, and by night I was working. We were awoken at 3 a.m. to help our parents clean a restaurant where my uncle found them a job.

We worked at the Moongate Cantonese Restaurant until I was sixteen, sweeping, mopping, scrubbing many nights, half-asleep, while my little brother slept in a booth. My father was again in his element of work. For me, it was hard being wakened, but even there I looked for the rainbow and found it in our ten-minute breaks. The restaurant had a piano, which, at those hours, was mine. While my parents rested, I would try to pick out songs on the keys, the first being "Que Sera, Sera" ("What*ever* will be, will be"). I was Doris Day, on my own stage. I was Lola Albright waiting for Peter Gunn, and I was Monica, singer and dancer of the Moongate.

In school I was not only sleepy but also lost in a sea of incomprehensible English. Classmates, who taught me strange words and then laughed when I repeated them, teased me. I was the little Dutch girl who wore the same dress every day and, in the sixth grade, still did not shave her legs. I spent much of my time quietly writing, copying what was on the blackboard, copying what was in the books. I would pinch myself black and blue, hoping all this were a dream, and I could make myself wake up in my own little bed, in my room with the balcony, on a street named for our queen.

But despite the pinches, I did not open my eyes back in Holland. I was always still in this classroom where the teacher's words were strange sounds.

As difficult as the adjustment was for me being in a strange school, it was more of a struggle for my parents. They felt isolated from mainstream U.S. culture, and people often looked on them as threatening for being different. *My father was courageous*, but maybe naive, in thinking that at over forty, with four children, he could start life over. He didn't know English, and he had no idea how large the country was. Every day he would venture out, walk by construction sites and, with his limited English, express that he wanted to work. I would hear him talking at night to Mama, telling her in Dutch, "I'd crawl back to Holland on my hands and knees."

She would listen and tell him, "Everything will be fine." Yet I knew it was even harder on her. She had never been away from her village. She'd try to keep his spirits up, hiding her own fears, as she did later with cancer. Mama had never worked, and now she was cleaning other people's homes, cleaning restaurants, ironing, baby-sitting. I could see the toll it took on her, the lines of sadness and regret in her face. They had their pride, though. Had they been able to give up and go back, they never would have. Then my sister was buried in U.S. soil, and the thought of going away was never discussed. They started learning English by listening to it. However, they still surrounded themselves with people from their own roots for comfort, talking and eating with friends in the Holland-American club. I had to do more than that. I must start to make sense of the teacher's sounds.

Eventually, however, I understood a few words. I decided to try them out, joining "home" with what sounded like "werk," to make "homework." I tried it on my new friend, Cheryl, who lived next door to my uncle and aunt. "*Do vee haf* homework?"

She answered right away, "Yes, we have homework." It worked. She hadn't laughed, just answered. I was not afraid to venture into these new waters. Then like pearls in a necklace, I joined words into sentences. We now had television, and I listened to Michael Landon talk English as he climbed on his horse in *Bonanza* and rode off into the mountains, probably not that far from my house.

In six months, I was speaking the language myself. Actually, Cheryl had been my friend before I spoke English. Even when she hadn't understood a word I said, she had smiled at me. We would swing alongside each other on the playground or go on walks mostly in silence. Little by little we were talking, sharing secrets like other young girls.

Prejudice Next Door

U nfortunately, not everyone was glad to see strangers in their neighborhood. Blinded by prejudice and fear, our own neighbors poured gasoline on our yard and set it afire, calling us dangerous communists. That Holland was not, nor ever had been, a communist country was not in their mental scope. It was a simple equation: Foreigners equal danger. The idea itself is what is dangerous in a country founded by people from other countries, joined with those already here.

Overcoming the ignorance of others and learning the language, I became a teenager, whose interests could follow a natural course. Now life had lessons far more difficult than a different language. There was illness, a new view of my mother and, finally, my *idea of love*.

The Pain of Loss

T he first began when I was thirteen, and my sister, Angeline, who was two years older, discovered she had a blister. It seemed harmless, but almost overnight it became very infected, and in a few weeks, my parents were told she had leukemia. During the next year, she lost sixty pounds! Despite her weakness, she kept her spirits up, even telling my parents not to worry. She was bedridden, and we would take turns reading to each other until one of us made a mistake. Sometimes I would ignore her mistake and stay because I loved hearing her voice. Violent coughing that made me cry inside with empathy, especially since I knew it hurt her abdominal surgery scar, would halt her reading. She had to have a colostomy, but she tried to joke about it, saying in Dutch, "At least I don't have to wipe my fanny."

Angeline was fun and optimistic until the end. When Papa went to see her in the UCLA hospital, he said she looked like an angel. My sister had been my best friend and yet it angered me that my father finally had something kind and loving to say when now it was too late. Young, beautiful Angeline took a piece of my heart when she left this world.

I remember riding in the limousine *and thinking, as we passed children in the schoolyard continuing to play ball,* "How can they keep on playing like that? How can they be having fun when we're taking my *sister*, my best friend, to be buried?"

In the San Fernando Cemetery the priest comforted us with the words, "God likes to be in good company. That's why the good die young."

That being true, I mused, *I'd certainly live a long, full life . . .*

Defeat Is Not My Future

Remembering Angeline, I continued to study. I
learned from the people around me, as well as in
school. I learned, watching the horrific riots in
Watts on TV, that we had to find a way for people to understand one another. I was learning also in my very home.
One night, when my mother was kissing me goodnight, I
saw her face as that of a woman, not just as my mother. She
was still young, in her forties, but she already looked sad and
disappointed. That scared me. I had seen that look of defeat
in the eyes of other women, too—her friends, ladies in the
stores; soon I termed it "the bitter woman look." I wanted
to ask her how it happened and, even more, how I could
make sure it never happened to me. I didn't ask because she
had become one of these women. I just kissed her goodnight, as I vowed it would not be part of my life. (It should-
n't be part of any woman's.) I was going to seek adventure,
keep my joy and find love. Actually, what I would take for
love was just around the corner.

III.

Take One:
A Dream of Love

A Peak at Tuscany

Meeting

L ove was around the corner, but I didn't know it. I was actually introduced to Jeffrey twice. The first time was by the athletic director, Mr. Ramirez. Sometime before, he had called me into his office and, smiling, surprised me with his announcement, "Monica, as you know, we're building a new football stadium, and I'm in charge of raising money to accomplish this. I was wondering if you'd pose with Dennis Sherman [our quarterback] in the local paper. I want you two to sit on the bleachers and hold a football."

I couldn't believe my ears. There were much prettier girls in school who wore beautiful clothes, not hand-me-downs from other people's homes like Mama brought home to me. (Some of the people for whom she worked had children in my school.) But Mr. Ramirez didn't want them; he wanted me. Me, who on weekends could be seen pushing a lawn-mower, with my best friend Carol carrying the rakes, going door to door offering our gardening services. "Yes, I will," I quickly replied before he could change his mind.

"Great. Just be on the field tomorrow at four. Don't worry about Mrs. Snyder. Her nose will be out of joint because I'm not picking one of her cheerleaders, but I want you."

"Thanks." Excitedly I ran out of the office, suddenly

bumping into a man who told me to slow down. I knew he wasn't old enough to be a teacher.

After I apologized, all he said to me was, "Don't ever stop smiling like that." He was cute and older.

When I asked my friend, Carol, if she'd seen him, she explained, "He's the student teacher for history." I knew he wasn't old enough to be a full teacher. He looked disheveled like he'd just come off the basketball court while wearing a sports coat.

At that time I wasn't going out with anyone. Mr. Ramirez's idea of the photos was even more of an honor because just the day before, I had been standing outside the schoolyard when Michael Ovitz drove by in his convertible sports car and asked casually, "Monica, who are you going to the prom with?"

I had answered, trying to sound just as casual, "I don't know yet." I couldn't tell a boy driving a sports car that I didn't have the money for a prom dress.

So the picture Mr. Ramirez requested appeared in the paper two days later. There I was, for the town to see, sitting on the bleachers smiling with Dennis next to me in his football uniform. Ms. Snyder berated me because the caption under the photo read, "Monica Reynders, Birmingham High School cheerleader, and Dennis Sherman . . ." Mr. Ramirez must have just told the newspaper that I was a cheerleader. In his eyes, I was, I guess.

Weeks later, someone told me I had been nominated for Carnival Queen, a festival sponsored by the men who supported the Booster Club, but it was pointed out that my father did not contribute money and was not a supporter of the athletic program, so my name was withdrawn. I suppose

I was pretty enough, but not rich enough. I never realized that I was remotely pretty, equating being tall with looking masculine, and when at times I complained to my mother that many of the girls treated me unkindly, she, without hesitation, informed me they were jealous. We were at a dance up at the lake (my first outing away from home), and my yellow pants were bloodstained, when a strange young man approached me and kindly told me, "Hey, I don't want to embarrass you, but the back of your pants are red, with blood." I ran upstairs and soaked the pants in cold water, put them back on and came downstairs with soaking wet yellow bell-bottoms, pretending I wasn't bothered by this embarrassing moment, not wanting to give my friends the satisfaction of the pain they had caused me. I never trusted them again. It hadn't been enough to see me embarrassed at the dance. They continued to harass me by taking my bra (the only one I had), stuffing it with peanut butter, and putting it in the freezer.

When I was helping in the refreshment stand at a football game, Mr. Ramirez introduced me to Jeffrey. I smiled, but I had already met Jeffrey at a party.

I had gone with my friend Debbie Jones to a "Welcome Home from Vietnam" celebration for Brian Gustafson. His mother had invited us. At that time, the war in Vietnam was far away, not a part of my protest feelings as it was later to become.

For this night we were having fun. We looked up and saw two young men come through the back door: Neil, who played football at the University of Tulsa, Oklahoma, and Jeffrey, who had been All City Quarterback at our high school and gone on to play for the University of Miami. I didn't know then all that lay in waiting for Jeffrey and me. Those at the party considered the two men heroes, but Jeffrey ignored me most of the night.

However, fate had a connection for us. Neil and Debbie were getting along already, and Neil invited us to go to another party with Jeffrey and him. We agreed and, during the trip, my wallet somehow was left in Neil's car. That started the process, for, of course, the next day they came by to return it. I invited Debbie to be part of the "returning." There he was in my house, a tall, very slender, broad-shouldered young man. He had thick, sandy brown hair and his eyes were green like mine. Jeffrey was the silent type, and I mistook his silence for intelligence. I later realized he just didn't have much to say. I also admired the way he did not pay much attention to me.

Then a month or two after that was Mr. Ramirez's introduction. He didn't know we'd already met. Jeffrey took my hand and asked, "Why haven't you called me?"

To which I replied, "I usually don't have to do the calling." We didn't go out then, but I asked him when his birthday was. He told me and, on September 18, I called to wish him a "happy birthday." He was pleased that I remembered, and this time he asked me for a date.

Beginnings of Love

W e'd go to the drive-in or out to dinner. Sometimes we'd go to his house and watch television. I was content then just to be with him. We didn't have deep conversations but just enjoyed each other's presence. I was falling in love, I thought, without knowing that much about him, nor about being in love. I found out later that even though he had been a quarterback in high school, he was known amongst his friends as one who kept to himself, rarely socializing with others. I wasn't analyzing him; I was just happy.

News

A ll of this dream-walking came face-to-face with reality ten months later when I discovered I was pregnant. Impossible, but I was. I couldn't bear to tell my parents, who got mad at me just for talking too long on the phone. And when at fourteen I had started my period, my mother demanded I not tell my father. Again, I was confused by her anger at me.

But I would tell them, and everything would be all right, because Jeffrey and I were in love. We would marry and live happily ever after. This is the way it was supposed to work in the 1960s, especially in the minds of young, religious girls.

Warming up, I first told my future sister-in-law, Paula, who was married to Jeffrey's brother. We were in stalls next to each other in the ladies' room at an LA Rams football game. Being eighteen also, and having just had a baby herself, she was supportive.

Next were my parents. My mother surprised me with her reply. "Monica, you don't have to marry him. Don't make two mistakes." This was from a Catholic mother, but perhaps it said something of her own views on marriage. Papa had nothing to say except the comment that he would arrange the church flowers if I decided to marry. *If?* "But I *want* to marry him," I pleaded. "I'm in love."

What did "I love him" mean at that age? Did it mean I wouldn't have to be home at eleven? Did it mean I could wear make-up and not have to wash it off when Papa was coming? Did it mean I could now talk on the phone when I wanted? Did it mean I wouldn't have Papa mad at me for growing up, always mad at me? It probably was all of these, plus liking to be with Jeffrey at movies or dinner. But I had no idea what life as a wife and soon-to-be mother meant. It was more about being independent and out of my parents' house. Yes, I would get married.

Now I had to tell his parents. They were equally skeptical, but worse. His father stated in a matter-of-fact way, while passing me a donut, "Monica, you know you don't have to marry Jeffrey. You don't even have to have the baby."

I gasped, unable to talk. My family was staunchly Catholic. When I regained speech, I was emphatic. "Sir, I **will** have this baby, whether your son and I are married or not. He can do what he wants, but I **will not** have an abortion."

I was more determined than ever to have my fantasy family. Looking back, I think my mother was right to encourage me to reconsider such a life-changing decision. Though I wouldn't trade those experiences for others, I believe no one should be allowed to marry at such a young and uninformed age. There should be a law that no one marries until at least the age of 25, though maybe that's still too young. The Catholic Church opposes divorce and makes it very difficult for those seeking one, yet they fail miserably at preparing young people for this major commitment. For this reason, they need to stop making people feel so guilty for failing at something they themselves don't understand.

Expectations

The Catholic Church requires counseling by a priest for all who wish to marry in the church, but the priests are incapable of guiding young people in all that being a husband or wife entails. I don't remember how the priest we saw counseled us. He was a kind man who seemed embarrassed as he spoke to us of sex within the confines of marriage. Priests are cloistered from worldly desires, yet they counsel those of us who are not. I do remember that the priest was married shortly after Jeffrey and me.

So, young and naïve, I took the vows, and my life of fantasy changed into reality rather quickly. In five years I became the mother of four children. In all, I have been married three times. While some may consider that record to be a failure, I consider it a great success. From each man whose life I shared, I always knew there was something to be learned, something to be gained. I still enjoy a warm friendship and a mutual respect with the father of my four children, almost forty years later. I wouldn't be known as "Mo Van, artist" (Van being part of my ex-husband's last name), if it weren't for my second marriage. Every experience is valuable, even those that don't go as hoped or planned. Each of my relationships came at a distinct and significant time in my life—a time of growth and flux. Of course, I wish I could have known all one needs to know the first time I said "I do." I knew that when things seemed dark or uncertain, God would help me make decisions that would carry me through to the *light.*

So now I was ready to start this experience of being married to Jeffrey. Each of us brought, as my parents had done in their marriage, our own ideas of what our roles should be. It wasn't something we discussed; we brought expectations silently, so problems were waiting for us.

IV.

New Years, New Lives

Wash Day

Four New Friends

From the beginning, my first baby, Dudley, was a dynamo, standing tall in his playpen, raring to go, ready to tackle any challenge. I'd take him outside and introduce him to nature, putting ladybugs and praying mantises in his hand. This love of the outdoors stayed with him years later when we ran a gardening business and remains with him now as he fishes and works in his greenhouse. I wanted to open the world to him, to give him the idea early that anything is possible if you imagine it, believe it. I was offering him a view of a free world, while my world was still constrained.

He came into the world while the Los Angeles Dodgers were beating the Atlanta Braves, on the first of September, 1967. The newspapers were talking of killings in Vietnam, classes on self-esteem in Head Starts, and a meeting of Arab nations to rid their countries forever of foreign bases. I was looking down at my new son, wanting him to have a life in a better world, a life with peace. I sang to him the familiar Dutch lullaby, changing the name to his, "*Ga nu slaapen, Dudley. Doe* je *oogjes nu sluiten.*" ("Go to sleep, Dudley. Close your little eyes.")

As a young wife, I thought my husband wanted perfection, although in reality I was bubbly, independent, and imperfect. He assumed I wanted a good provider and a strong leader. We didn't assign those roles to each other; we just played them, with word-perfect accuracy and skill. And so, the babies continued to arrive. I took the role of mother seriously, but at the same time I was finding the *me*, a closet hippie. *As soon as Jeffrey left to manage a department store*, I'd put on a braided leather headband, put on my Jefferson Airplane album and dance around the room.

More children to dance with were added every other year. Months before the moon landing, Laura arrived, a green-eyed beauty, with dark hair that soon turned blond. She was also born with optimism. She fought to play baseball on a boy's team, and was one of the *first girls to ever play* on the *boys' All Star team*. She had tenacity for reaching her goals from the start. Children have to seek their dreams, not ours.

While Laura and Dudley were still babies, we experienced our world shake, literally, with the earthquake of 1971. Jeffrey grabbed Laura, and I Dudley, and we rushed outside. I thought it was lucky there was no third child because there was no one else to grab another baby. What I didn't know was I was already pregnant with my third, Kristen.

Like the earthquake that she felt before arriving, Kristen (later nicknamed Fee by her nephews) has always been lively and exciting. As a toddler, she wanted to make new life happen, so she planted a little garden of carrots and prayed each night that they would come up. I was teaching her the value of prayer and faith. However, despite her petitions, nothing happened to the carrot seeds. Not wanting to squelch her enthusiasm, I put full-grown carrots for her to proudly pick and take to Show and Tell. Of course, my gardener, young Dudley, had to point out that I had put the carrots in upside down. Kristen also yearned to be on television. At only five years old, she'd called the **Gong Show** (a forerunner of **American Idol**) long distance to apply.

Since my vocation was now motherhood, as well as trying to fit my role of wife, I went at it full-time. Music was always a part of this mix. We sang and danced to Fleetwood Mac, Jose Feliciano, and the Stones. I would whirl the latest baby around *on my hip* as I crooned the "Mockingbird" song.

Singing, hugging, and dancing were my favorite parts. I enjoyed the moment and the individual personalities of these new people who were my circle. I also tackled the rest, cleaning, cooking, washing diapers and hanging them in the sun. More importantly, I had fun. Children can sense what's done in love.

All the while, around us news was arriving by television and the **LA Times**. Young men were needlessly being blown up in Vietnam. Jeffrey didn't have to go because he was a husband and a father by the time his draft notice arrived, but I knew people who went. A friend had a good-bye party for her son leaving for the war. Three weeks later he came home in a box. What a waste. I could see why people were marching in the streets and singing, "Where Have All the Young Men Gone?" Being against the war was as natural a part of me as loving my children. I felt the mothers on both sides of the battle loved their children just as much as I did. No child should have to grow up in a country at war. They are peace personified, our future.

Nixon was on television telling us we needed to be in Vietnam, but he wasn't sending a child. Young students at Kent State marched peacefully toward soldiers, putting flowers in the barrels of their guns, and were sometimes shot at. Martin Luther King spoke against the war, and was condemned. I thought, ***if people could just learn the simple truths of love, forgiveness, and respecting differences, there would be no wars. As long as people have prejudices and build borders between us, there will be war.*** I could only bring those ideas to my world and pray. News anchors brought reality.

In the midst of this news, there were bright spots on television, too. Lucy and Carol Burnett kept us laughing, and women were working their magic. On ***Bewitched*** and ***I Dream of Jeannie*** they were showing power, a freedom of expression, though only in make-believe. I tried my hand at painting, enjoying the colors blending together on a canvas, feeling the exhilaration, but I soon turned to the more practical art of sewing. I bought a sewing machine at a yard sale and taught myself through trial and error. Soon I had made clothes for the children, shirts for Jeffrey, and, to go with my peace posters, I made myself peasant blouses and full skirts. Soon I was sewing for eight boutiques on Ventura Boulevard, buying fabrics at outlets. My sister-in-law joined me in creating, and we'd drive by to see our clothes on display. An outfit I'd sold them for $35 sold for $75 or $150.

In my universe, I was creating a haven of tranquility, hard work and love. Yet I was also worn out from all my domesticity. With children, the other side of exhilaration is exhaustion. My mother offered to watch the children so I could visit my Holland and see my beloved grandmother. However, I decided to go to the doctor for a last-minute check-up before the trip. After the three babies in four years, I had decided that despite attending Catholic mass on Sundays, I needed to think of myself and the three children who needed my attention. I had asked the doctor to fit me with an IUD. Jeffrey was not a practicing Catholic, so he had no objection. So it was to my great surprise when the doctor called with the results of my "check-up": I was pregnant. (The IUD came out with the baby.)

I was overwhelmed at the thought of caring for another, but, of course, **not** having the baby was never considered. As we walked, pushing two babies in a stroller, and little Dudley walking by us, a neighbor thrust in my hand a book, **Population Explosion**. It was a little late. This baby was going to arrive. (The same neighbor welcomed triplets not less than a year later and another baby shortly thereafter; God is good!)

And she did. Andrea (Aunnie), my little angel, arrived with the peace treaty in Vietnam. With my youngest in my arms, we watched as U.S. prisoners finally returned, limping down airplane steps to waiting embraces and tears of joy. Born to a world now at peace, she was the cream on my coffee, a bright star. (Today, at six feet tall, Aunnie still brightens the world around her.) At a young age, she also liked to play baseball. Once in the snow, she was running from second to third, and I signaled to just **slide**. Today we sign our letters with love and a hand signaling, "Just let it slide." It's our signal to overcome whatever life brings.

With my four young children, I dedicated myself to coaching soccer, working at the snack stand, going to parent-teacher conferences. They gave me a joy I knew deep down I could have, but had never known. I decorated the walls with posters of love poems and, when Jeffrey wasn't home, I ended most sentences with "peace." My gregariousness and vitality contrasted with Jeffrey's need for solitude.

The children and I were his opposite. We thrived on meeting people of all races, countries, and occupations, including a president.

The latter happened when Andrea was about four, and I was driving her home from a park. Every now and then she would look at me and smile. I sang, slightly off-key, "The Itsy-Bitsy Spider," and she made the motions with her hands of the spider climbing the spout.

As we passed the Shore Cliff Golf Course in San Clemente, something, or should I say **someone,** caught my eye. I made a quick U-turn and brought my beat-up 1967 Ford Mustang to a screeching halt between the eighth and ninth holes. I turned to Andrea, "I'll be right back. You stay here." I jumped out of the car and skipped toward a middle-aged gray-haired man leaning against his Ford LTD station wagon. It was green, with fake wood siding, and parked on the wrong side of the street. He was casually looking over his shoulder.

"Is he who I think he is?" I asked, pointing to one of two gentlemen carrying golf bags on the fairway.

"Yep," the man replied, unfazed, still leaning on the hood.

"Are you the Secret Service?"

"Yep."

"Is it okay if I say hello?"

"Sure." I smiled back at the man as I made my way toward the golfing strangers. Richard Nixon put down his club at my approach, shook my hand, and introduced me to his son-in-law, David. I looked over and waved at Andrea as Nixon and I walked toward my car. She took her two fingers out of her mouth and hid her **kankie** under the seat before rolling down the window.

"Andrea, I want you to meet Mr. Nixon. He was the President of the United States just a few years ago."

"Hello, Andrea," he spoke kindly. Then he looked at me.

"Are those her permanent teeth?" He seemed genuinely concerned.

"No, they're just her baby teeth. I pray every night God will be so good as to send her permanent teeth that are straight." He looked at the ripped headliner of my classic Mustang, perhaps thinking that prayer was probably my only chance for aligned teeth.

"I had terribly crooked teeth as a young man. Pat only agreed to marry me on the condition that I have my teeth fixed, so I did." I marveled that President Nixon and I were talking as old friends, and about teeth, of all subjects. He told me he had just become a grandfather for the first time. He asked me how to say "Merry Christmas" and "Happy New Year" in Dutch. He said he had signed his book, *Memoirs*, like that for someone from Holland. I told him I'd bought an autographed copy of his book in San Juan Capistrano. We discussed restaurants, and he said his favorite was El Adobe. All the time we chatted, David stayed behind, practicing his swing.

Every now and then I'll pick up the signed copy of President Nixon's book, *Memoirs*, from my bookshelf and remember jumping back into the Mustang and telling Andrea, "Don't ever forget this day, but more than that, never be afraid. If you ever are, just ask yourself, 'What's the worse thing that can happen?'"

It was an extraordinary day for Andrea and me, which we still remember. I tried to give each child time when it was just the two of us. Parenting was my vocation but, like all parents, I sometimes wished I had a day off.

❋ ❋ ❋

I went with my sister-in-law to New York City, where we

were actually not with children. Before I left, I asked each one what he or she wanted me to bring back. Dudley, like the girl who asked for the rose in **Beauty and the Beast**, had a simple request—just a baseball with the signatures of all the players of the New York Mets. He might as well have asked for a piece of the moon. I put it down as what I *wished* I could do. But when we went to Ponti's, a restaurant in Little Italy, Joe Torre was there and knew my sister-in-laws' friends. He made the dream come true—a ball with all the signatures and a cap, too. That same night I met and danced with David Kennedy, son of Robert. As we were dancing at a club called Xenons I remembered how I had met his father, Robert Kennedy, at Valley College shortly before he was assassinated in 1968. David, ignoring the fact that I was married, requested my phone number so he could come out and visit in California. I had to go home. It was an eye-opening trip. Drugs of every kind were being offered in a private section of the club called "the inspiration room." David was intrigued because my sister-in-law and I both declined politely. When someone offered me something illegal, he would tell him or her to get lost because "she doesn't do that shit." He was protective of me for the short time we were together with friends at the club. He was young and kind and told me he would think of me whenever he heard Waylon Jennings' song "I Can Get Off on You," a song about a man who is addicted to booze and drugs, but then he meets a girl, and doesn't need anything but her. It was wishful thinking on his part, as he was so young and seemingly lost. It came as no surprise to me when I read he had died of a drug overdose in Palm Beach in 1984. I was glad to be back with my children, back in my simple world.

Yet sometimes, in a flash, the thought of escape would

pass my mind, and then melt. One such day happened when I had just said good-bye to my children as they climbed on the yellow school bus and rode off. I turned and saw a white van approaching. The van stopped for a moment, at the corner of Yolanda and Kittridge Streets. The driver glanced my way. I recognized the Black man behind the wheel and the woman sitting beside him. Their picture had been on every front page of the newspaper for weeks. I purposely walked slower than normal and for a brief *moment* imagined them taking me with them, like they had Patti, if only just around the corner. But they made a right turn and disappeared. Later, when I went to the local butcher, he informed me how Willie Cinque (who took his name from a rebel slave was actually an escaped convict who was obsessed with weapons and was a lifelong loser in battles with the law. The SLA emerged in Berkeley in 1971, led by a gang of young, White, well-educated middle-class zealots who pledged to stamp out competition, individualism, racism, sexism and capitalism. The core message that the country was racist and controlled by corporate interest seems today like old news); and the rest of the SLA members, with Patti Hearst, had bought New York steaks there at the local butcher's on Reseda Boulevard. I sighed and asked for my ground round. It was Tuesday, and that meant meatballs, spinach and potatoes. For one minute I imagined I had gone away with the SLA, imagining what it must have been like for Patti as they stormed her room and took her while demanding four million dollars and then upping the ante to six million for her safe return. I felt stifled in my lifeless marriage. I wanted to fly away like a bird, with Peter Pan to Never Never Land. Instead, I went home and made meatballs. For hundreds of more Tuesdays, I made meatballs, rather than taking the children and leaving, but the seed of the idea was there.

While raising young children, it seemed to me that certain truths existed. I thought of a few of them.

PARENTING

YOU CAN BE THE GREATEST PARENT, BUT YOUR CHILDREN WILL DO A BETTER JOB PARENTING. THEY WILL TELL YOU SO, AND YOU WISH THEM LUCK.

❈   ❈   ❈

YOU CAN GIVE YOUR CHILDREN TOO LITTLE, AND THEY WILL COMPLAIN OF NOT GETTING ENOUGH. YOU CAN GIVE THEM TOO MUCH, AND THEY WILL CHASTISE YOU FOR HAVING MADE IT TOO EASY FOR THEM.

❈   ❈   ❈

STEPCHILDREN LIKE THEIR STEPFATHERS BETTER THAN THEIR STEPMOTHERS.

❈   ❈   ❈

RICH STEPCHILDREN WOULD LIKE THEIR STEPMOTHERS BETTER IF THEIR FATHERS WEREN'T RICH.

❈   ❈   ❈

ONE DAY YOUR CHILDREN LOOK AT YOU AND THINK YOU'RE GETTING OLD.

❈   ❈   ❈

ONE DAY YOUR CHILDREN WILL LOOK IN THE MIRROR AND REALIZE THEY'RE GETTING OLDER.

❈   ❈   ❈

Wake Up, Little Susie

But while the children and I had a microworld that was spinning in the right galaxy, the threads of marriage I was sewing were coming apart, and neither Jeffrey nor I wanted to see that. We each were different individuals, parts of different puzzles that did not fit. When he came home from work, he went straight to the bedroom and read his paper until I announced that dinner was on the table. While I was eager to rush and tell him what each child had done or show him a newly sewn child's outfit, he sought silence and solitude. I told him once that my being married to him was like my peeing in the ocean. It made no difference. I didn't feel a connection. Thoughts of leaving appeared again, but disappeared as quickly. I didn't have the nerve, and there was always my religion.

Our incompatibility became most evident one night when we went with friends to see the musical *Hair* at a Hollywood theater. The show was about war and peace, love and life, and being free to be. This was my mantra, be free to be yourself. That show touched me, and I felt it physically as well as spiritually. At the end, I stood up as the cast rallied out into the audience, encouraging us to join in the finale. Only the "grooviest" of audience members joined, I being one of them. United in the power of the music, we sang "Aquarius" and "Let the Sun Shine In." We filled the auditorium with joyful sounds.

Jeffrey did not join in. In fact, he was so embarrassed by my participation that he refused to speak to me for a week. But not even his reproach could have kept me from lifting my voice with that antiwar hippie group. I was one with them.

Even in the silence, we continued our charade, until cracks in our facade began to reveal that which we could no longer hold back, our real selves breaking through to the open air. Irreparably, the cracks gave way to crumbling walls that eventually tumbled into the sea.

In my time of indecision, I looked for other couples who looked like they had perfect relationships. I found one at church. We used to sit behind a lovely couple at St. Edward's Catholic Church in Dana Point. Often I would marvel at the back of the woman's head. When I should have been praying or paying attention to the homily, I would wonder how she got that French braid so perfectly straight. Unconsciously, my hand would go to my own hair. I had been trying to learn to French-braid my hair like hers, but with four kids running around, there was barely time to comb it. Week after week, the stunning blonde sat next to her star-athlete husband, distracting me from my prayers. Perhaps I did look at them with a touch of envy. They were young and beautiful, seemingly happy and seemingly in love. As I sat with my disenchanted husband and four children, I felt a sense of shame.

Earlier that week, while I was teaching fifth-grade church

CCD class, my face grew hot as we turned in our primers to the chapter on **matrimony**. I was no longer sure I believed all I had been taught by the Church, my parents, and even by my own experience. How could I tell impressionable young children about marriage, when mine was falling apart? I told the students to skip to the **forgiveness** chapter, hoping they wouldn't notice.

"Teacher," a young boy asked, "what about chapter seven?" I just smiled.

"It's more important that we talk about forgiveness," I said, secretly hoping God could forgive me for my doubts.

I knew my marriage was hanging by a thread, that I was questioning our future together. Looking at the attractive couple in front of me, I imagined their happiness, their love, and their wonderful life. Again, I asked God to forgive me for being ungrateful.

"Mom, may I get his autograph after mass?" my seven-year-old son whispered, breaking my trance. I had no idea who the man was, but I saw my husband was also a fan.

"Sure, son," Jeffrey answered. "We'll ask him after the service."

While the gregarious athlete happily signed my son's slip of paper, I smiled and wondered at the blessings that had put this perfect couple together. She was a sun-kissed beauty with perfectly braided hair, and he was so handsome: broad-shouldered with perfect teeth and smooth, ebony skin. They seemed to have it all. Years later, we were all glued to the television as the police chased his white Bronco through L.A. She was dead.

There was no sense to be made in O.J. and Nicole's violent end, but I still held on to hope for my marriage. People were making it work. I was determined to be one of them. I asked God for his guidance. I knew if I trusted in Him, He would reveal his plan for my life. I had to be patient.

Years passed, but the gulf between Jeffrey and me widened. The decision to leave was now more than just a seed; it was ready to sprout. It reached light one night during a school open house. I looked around the room and realized that many of the parents there were living lies. They were no happier than Jeffrey and I, but they were hidden behind faces of false happiness. I knew many were involved in affairs, men as well as women, hoping to feel closer to love. That might work for them, but it was not for me. Seeing them, I knew what I had to do for my own life.

I knew then that Jeffrey and I could no longer play the roles we had chosen for ourselves. The fantasy was shattered and reality took hold. The notion of love to which I had been so desperately clinging was nothing more than a romantic cloud. What I came to understand was that a dream-life is intangible; you can't hold it in your hands, and no matter how much you want it to be real, it vanishes like the mist when the sun rises. I explained incompatibility to the children, as I believe in being honest with them. Surely they had already noticed.

So, one cool, breezy Monday morning, I woke up with the sun and prepared myself to meet the day and face my waking life. Scrubbed and dressed, I made breakfast for Jeffrey. Nothing seemed out of the ordinary as I poured his coffee.

"I think I'll head up to Tahoe for the summer. I'll take the kids, and we can see how it works." Without looking up from his paper, he nodded his approval.

"Maybe you could buy a house there. It would be a good investment." His manner was cool and businesslike. There was no begging, no pleading, no wailing. Practical to a fault, he agreed and went about his morning. If he had once said, "Please, Monica, stay," I might have. Instead, he left for work, and I started packing.

Four children and fourteen years after our traditional Catholic wedding, I drove my kids to Lake Tahoe, and never looked back.

❄ ❄ ❄

V.

Wings of My Own

Peak of Paradise

When I finally reached my decision and started driving them north, my children could feel my exuberance at being free. We sang our repertoire of songs, but with new feeling. We ran through "Sunshine on My Shoulder" and "I'm Leaving on a Jet Plane," our favorite that starts, "In the morning when I rise," as the road went higher, leading us to pine-covered mountains.

Many women look for the nerve to finally leave a situation that does not work for them. For some it's escaping physical or verbal abuse, for others it's leaving a lack of communication that breeds emptiness. Some have to run in the middle of the night with only the clothes on their backs. The organization, WINGS (Women in Need of Growing Stronger), helps women such as those, and because I empathize, I always donate a painting to their fundraising. Although I was never physically abused, I understand their need to get away. Everyone should be able to live in peace and with whom they wish. Some need help when they find *the desire to change their situation.*

For me, choosing the right time and finding the courage to search for a new life came when circumstances were right. A friend of mine, Jodie, who had four children, too, had a large house near Tahoe. Her husband worked out of town and came home only rarely. She had invited us to stay awhile. Also, my Ome Jerry and Tante Alie lived in Tahoe. The town offered a refuge.

So with the pieces in place, I drove in the summer sun toward Tahoe. All around us, the compelling pristine beauty pulled us toward a celestial calm.

Calm until Jodie and I found jobs in a casino and saw a life we had never experienced. Before finding work, we settled into

Jodie's cabin, a place with mountains outside the windows. I walked outside and imagined them covered with snow like in Holland. Yes, my children and I could be happy here.

First and foremost among my priorities was making them feel at home. Whatever job I took, from the casinos to a florist shop, I made sure it was one where I could be home when they were. As soon as school started, I had them enrolled, and with their natural gregarious ways, they made friends, often bringing them to our fun-filled house. I had cookies and lemonade in the fall, hot chocolate, ghost stories and even a joke or two in the winter, and always music: Neil Young, Starship, Fitzgerald, Dylan, and the Beatles. It was my life now, so I could turn up the volume and enjoy each day as I saw fit. Years later, some of them would call me, considering me a second mom. One morning, I woke early to have a few minutes alone with my coffee and relax before starting to work. I packed four lunches and put out four envelopes of money for school photos. When I was married, I would have selected the full package of photos for each one, but now I had to conform to the smallest. An extra three dollars each, twelve in total, was not always easy to have. But it didn't matter because many years later, my son sent me a letter making it real clear that lack of money or luxuries during our time in Tahoe had never been an issue. I am sure that, at the time, I had wished that I could have given them more—more brand-name clothes, trips, and the most expensive school picture package. From that letter he sent me many years later, I realized that all my sleepless nights worrying about money, keeping it all together, and making sure the kids didn't do without—my concerns that seemed warranted at the time—had not been necessary.

PLAIN OLD: My son remembers the sweetness of just "plain old."

Mom,

You taught me to sing "Band on the Run" (Beatles), in the old green Datsun. "Well the rain came down with a mighty crash as we headed towards the sun, the first one said to the second one there I hope you're having fun."

Elena was on the trampoline, and she said, "Let's plain old jump," and she bounced up and down with exuberance. I wondered how she learned that phrase. I almost felt tears as I thought of our "plain old" days of times past. To think, my four-year-old just wanted something "plain old" even if it were just with her dad.

When I look back and remember the things I experienced with you, I think of "plain old" as being something really good. I guess that's why I like plain old bikes, mirrors, doors, women, and so many other things. I like plain old fishing, working in the garden, painting, and respect for my elders and fellow man and woman. Nothing is "plain old" anymore. You taught that simpleness is when you find peace. Sharing smiles, laughs, goodness, a plain old desire that your friends and those around you are "plain old happy." That even though things are so fucking complicated, the plain oldness of yesterday will get us through today, till tomorrow. I just want to thank you for my plain old heart.

From the earliest of times I remember you and Pam making clothes, you putting pictures on bottles, transforming the bottle into a piece of art. How you introduced me to nature by putting a praying mantis on my back and hearing you say, "They must really like you, there is one on your back." Putting leaves in my hands so I could feel the texture and an intense desire that I as your child relish in nature as it is so complete, and never differentiating between a weed and a flower. You saw beauty in everything. I think what makes you so great is your patience to make sure we all had everything we needed. Not just things, but love of good company, love of the sea, the lake, and big waves, camping in our little tent. Plain old simple things. Happy times, later finding out that in your native tongue there is a name for it: gezellig. A great word, and there is no English translation for it. And I am so glad my mother knew how to create that feeling. I love that word. It's funny how understanding these things was brought on by a young woman's desire to love her children and see them happy. You tried as hard as anyone and still do. It is being playful, but not being played with. It's being loved, not allowing others to hate; it's being open with one another, knowing nothing could ever be that bad. It's plain old understanding.

Accepting people for who they are and not their skin color. You taught that just by your actions. I never felt prejudice till I moved to Tennessee. Thanks, for not letting me understand prejudice. Fresh flowers, on the tabletops, even when I knew you couldn't afford them. You didn't know that I knew you would go to the flower shop in Incline and get the old ones, because they still had life left in them, and be largely discounted. I knew.

Mocking Bird. Yeah, have you heard he's gonna buy me a mockingbird, and if that mockingbird don't sing he's gonna buy me that diamond ring. I remember laughing, listening to your songs. You never got the words quite right, with your one deaf ear, but you sang and made up words as you sang along. Linda Rondstadt. Hearing Neil Young for the first time in Tahoe. You took us places, the greatest places in our mind. Always rely on that forwardness that never kept you down. It was all just "plain, old" fun.

Your son, Dudley

❃ ❃ ❃

I went to work a little weary that morning. I was working with Jodie as a hostess in the casino, welcoming people to a place I didn't know myself. I had never been around gambling and so much alcohol. Employees would have mood swings induced, which we, being so naïve, didn't realize were caused by drugs. I just concentrated on my job and caring for my children, with some support Jeffrey sent.

Jodie and I were not casino people, but we were hardworking.

It was a real awakening to be working in that unfamiliar world. Often I'd see the same faces weekend after weekend. People came up from the Bay area, trying to win money with money they couldn't afford to lose. Casino employees took their paychecks and within minutes were sitting at the tables. In just a few more minutes, they would leave broke, having to wait another week for pay.

It was a tempting situation. Sometimes I would get up early in the morning and go over to another casino with a hundred dollars and play blackjack. I would play until I was ahead by no less than $80 and go home. I did this for almost a year, and it helped pay for ski passes, ski clothes and other extras. Then one day I decided that if I could do this with a hundred dollars, I could do it just as easy with a thousand.

I sat down and was ready to win all the money I needed for "back-to-school" clothes. Or so I thought.

After one hand, I was ahead two hundred, then four hundred dollars, but in a short time everything changed. I was busted. I felt sick, so sick all over that I never again put another penny on the tables. It had been fun and exciting, but losing the one thousand cured me forever. I knew then that work was the only answer. I worked sometimes three jobs at a time, and I gave my all to doing a good job at the casino.

The result was that I was soon made manager, and later moved to sales. I was able to buy a small townhouse of my own, with no money down. I filled the tables with plants and magazines and the walls with photographs and prints. Whenever I wanted, I could light a fire in the fireplace with no one complaining of the heat or the cost. I was in control of my own territory. It was my own Fourth of July. I sunbathed on the deck in my bikini and took the children to hike beneath the forests, as a little girl in Holland had once done. We shared our love of nature.

That winter I worked at the casino, flower shop and sometimes at a Chinese restaurant, providing us with a bit more money. I was able to buy us season ski passes for Incline Village Ski Resort and took advantage of living in the mountains. The first time we rode the ski lift, the children were in the chairs behind me. Just as we were coming down, they shouted in unison, "Look at Mom, look at Mom," and then, "Look at Mom fall." I tumbled in the snow, skis in the air, face in the snow, unable to get up. They all laughed, and I did too, thinking how I must look.

They pulled me up and dusted me, but they wanted to

go back up the mountain. I was ready for hot chocolate in the ski lodge. Once inside, I finally warmed up near the fire, with its blue lights from the pinecones. I took off my gloves and ordered a coffee drink. Just sitting there, enjoying the fire, the wind burning on my face, looking out of the window at my children, and thanking God, for all my blessings that day. Just being content, at not having broken any bones.

Working in a casino restaurant was demanding, but it had its perks, too. By way of a friend, I was invited to sit next to Frank Sinatra one night—a long way from the shy young girl who had passed through his Hoboken on the way from Holland. Just before meeting Frank, I was seated next to Loretta Lynn, a singer I so admire. I was surprised to hear her say that *she* was nervous about meeting Frank. Whatever for? Loretta was so famous herself. I have the memories from that evening, and my daughter, Laura, has the music box I was given that plays "My Way."

In that job, I was in a new life where I could think beyond the basics. And one particular morning, someone else was thinking beyond the basics. It made me realize that leaving with four children isn't something I would recommend to everyone, but it was the right thing for us. It wasn't long after we had moved to Lake Tahoe that Jeffrey decided to relocate to Reno, twenty-six miles away from us. We continued as friends, sharing time with the children, and never creating any animosity between us. Never did we speak unkindly of each other, and we were always united in decisions pertaining to the children.

I had just sent the children off to school, had my usual cup of coffee and was cleaning cold cereal off the floor when the phone rang.

"Are you Monica?"

"Yes, and with whom am I speaking?"

He remained nameless and went right to the point, "Have you ever made love on the telephone?"

"What? Have I ever *what*?" Was I really hearing this? Not only had I never made love on the telephone, I hadn't made love in almost a year. I wasn't sure what to say next, but I went to the truth. "Look, mister. I'm on my hands and knees, clearing up Cheerios, my left roller just fell out of my hair, and . . ."

"Hey, lady, forget it. I might be perverted, but no way do I want to make love to you while you're wiping the floor."

Strange, but I thought I'd play along for a minute. "I could take the rollers out, and the floor can wait . . ."

"Listen, I just picked your name out of the phone book. I didn't know you had kids. You should serve them something besides cold cereal."

He was not only weird but also insulting, but all in fun I presumed. "I usually fix them French toast or pancakes, but we were in a rush this morning. I did fix them a good lunch, though."

"Look, lady, I'm sorry to bother you. You're really nice, not the sort of chick who needs an idiot *like me* calling her like this. My old lady never even got out of bed in the morning to give us anything. And then one day she split. I mean she didn't even say good-bye. Can you believe a mother would just split like that? Like what did we do? We were only six and nine. I don't even know where my brother is. I mean I never saw her again. Never did know my old man." He was silent. "Anyway, sorry I bothered you. I never

thought I'd reach a mother. Don't ever split on your kids."
And he hung up.

Split on my kids? The idea had never occurred to me. I
couldn't even imagine it, but, sadly, I knew there must be
those who did.

I went back to my coffee, which now needed reheating.
The conversation was bizarre, but it *was* with another adult.
I realized that most of my talking had been with children or
customers, and I had complained before of wanting communication. So, when I met Charlie, and he took an interest in me, the attention was welcome. My girlfriend and I
went to a restaurant called Goldstein's in Incline Village. At
about 10 p.m. a group of college kids came in. One was
wearing a heavy knit Irish sweater and reminded me of
David Kennedy. He was introduced as Charlie, and he was
twenty-three to my thirty-two, but we were attracted to each
other right away. He asked me to dance, and we were
together for four years. It was very special, yet in the back of
my mind, I always felt we would go separate ways. I knew
he would want to have children of his own, and he eventually did. While we were together, though, he was great with
my children. He would play his acoustic guitar, and we'd
sing. If the electricity went off, we would all huddle together, kids, Mom, and Charlie, and sing in the dark. We shared
a love of the outdoors, and for the first time in my life, I felt
completely comfortable just being myself. I was living the
youth I had missed. Sometimes, we'd drive in a beat-up
truck to a casino to try for the million-dollar jackpot. All the
way, we'd talk about how we'd spend the money. We never
won, of course, but the trip and the dreams were worth it.

His philosophy on life and love was summed up for me

on a trip to a snowy mountain. We hiked with our dog Rupert trailing behind, occasionally stopping to wallow in the snow. A light flurry was falling, and the towering pines swayed in the breeze. Suddenly Charlie embraced me from behind. He swung me around, and we fell laughing into a bank under the canopy of green. "Monica, I love you so much," he whispered. "Remember this moment." I looked to the sky and felt the kisses of snowflakes on my face and Charlie's kisses on my neck. As we lay in the snow bank, I rolled his words around in my mind. Life is made of millions of flakes, each one special. A life is made of moments, each one precious on its own. Combined with a million others, it's complete.

I never did forget that moment. Charlie reminded me that the beauty of life is not in the details. Eventually we parted ways, taking with us this memory.

In the middle of dating Charlie, when he took a hiatus of a few weeks, I was courted by Saul. His ex-wife had worked for me, and she introduced us. He immediately took my hand and walked me through the casino, but I pulled it away. He was moving too quickly.

I did date him awhile, but I told him that if my former boyfriend called again, I'd go back. Saul didn't seem to mind, confident he could win me over. He took me riding in his Mercedes and to stores to try on fur coats. He said he would be happy to "keep" me, lavishing me with whatever money could buy, but although it was flattering, I knew there was not that much between us.

Having left a relationship with little in common, I did not want another, regardless of any fringe benefits. I told him that I couldn't imagine his being at home with my children and me watching **Little House on the Prairie**. He insisted he could do anything to be with me, but I knew that was not his style. He had more worldly interests. I had once written a paper about "Need vs. Greed," which seemed to fit now. "We need to eat, but we don't need dessert. We need to love, but when we get possessive or demanding, it's greed. Need is wearing shoes so one doesn't hurt his feet walking on the hard pavement. Greed is wearing one-hundred-dollar Gucci shoes while one's brother is walking barefoot." I didn't want to be in a world of greed, although Saul and I would remain friends as long as he lived. I'd wait for Charlie's phone call.

And while I waited, I talked over love and life with my new friend, Lara. I told her about both Charlie and Saul, and all my concerns of being a single mother. "It would be so simple, Lara, to just sail into the sunset with Saul, giving the children the private tutors he offered, cruising the world in a yacht. But I'm in love with a pizza cook, so what can I do but wait."

"I know. *I met* a man in Dana Point who is everything I want. He's a surfer with three little boys. He's really nice, good-looking and just wished he didn't live so far away."

"Okay, so what's the catch?"

"He's married." This brought it all home to me, not wanting to live a life of pretense. I often wondered how many women stay in marriages knowing their husbands are unfaithful, yet they wouldn't want to let go of all the fringe benefits of being the wife. How many women close their eyes knowing, and in some cases relieved, that her man is getting it elsewhere? No, I'd wait and see if Charlie called. Sometimes while I'm returning to Orange County, thoughts of the surfer, the man my friend had told me about, would enter my mind, and I'd wonder if they had ended up together. Eventually, the phone did ring. I returned to Charlie, and we enjoyed each other and our time together. After trips to Southern California, I decided to move back. Charlie followed, and we started a gardening business together. I knew it wasn't a "forever" thing. Someday he would want children of his own, and I was past that.

For now, we would enjoy what California and being together had to offer.

VI.

Back Down South

Laguna Afternoon

My move to Southern California was the result of a few things. For one, Tahoe was not really the place to raise children or to work. It was hard to live there unless you were wealthy. Most of the jobs were in casinos, and they had the backdrops of alcohol and drugs. I was offered a completely different job, that of buyer of Italian linens. My early years of designing and sewing for boutiques had made an impression on the woman doing the hiring for this titillating job. It could have been fun for someone. I was sent to Italy with expenses. But this was not the job for a mother. Instead of enjoying myself, I was constantly missing the children. I went home, resigned, and headed south.

I had a few tools, a mower, a truck with a ramp, and determination. All the mowing and yard work I had done as a teenager had prepared me for this new vocation. It was hard physical work to mow lawns and plant flowers, but I was home when the children were, and it was close to nature. People would ask where I got my buffed arms and I would say, "In La Costa," not mentioning that I meant gardening, pulling weeds and hauling dirt; working, not working out at the famous La Costa Spa. It was then that I realized that it is all in the presentation. Charlie and I continued together in both gardening and at home for a while, but I knew we would be temporary, and we were. He left, married, and had three children; but our time, like a snowflake, was a time of beauty.

My children and I had a rented home in Cardiff-by-the-Sea, near the beach.

I continued the business, and Dudley, my teenage son, became my partner when he was not in school. I took time to enjoy life solo. I met many people with the yard work.

One friend I met was Nancee. Once my daughter babysat for her, and when she brought Andrea home, Nancee stayed and talked until four in the morning. We became friends, and I discovered that although she had a big, beautiful house, and I was a struggling mother with four children, she envied *me*. She envied my freedom, and my guts to do things on my own. I learned you have to build the life that works for you.

I met another friend soon after that. She worried about me, "You don't have any savings, social security. You don't live in the real world."

I smiled, admitting I didn't. My life worked for me and still does.

In another conversation, Nancee discovered that I had traveled on the ***Ryndam*** as an immigrant, and told me she had taken the ***Ryndam*** on a world cruise. We enjoyed the coincidence. Here we were together, having coffee, sharing our feelings. I felt content with my life alone, for then, but always in the back of my mind, I hoped someday I'd meet the man whose ideas and ideals matched mine.

Meanwhile, I continued my studies of what makes two people happy together by dating other men. I also remembered couples I'd seen. I think each couple figures out what works for them.

I remember a couple I saw one night while driving from Lake Tahoe to Orange County. I stopped off at an old cowboy establishment. The place was straight out of a movie, dimly lit with red neon beer signs flickering above the bar. Peanut shells crunched under our feet as we took a table near the dance floor. The band played country music and couples two-stepped to the twang. An older couple caught my eye. They were in their late sixties, and they laughed as they shuffled and spun around the floor. I was mesmerized. That's what I wanted in life—a dance partner.

Later I saw the female half of the dancing couple in the ladies' room. As we dried our hands, I told her, "I really enjoyed your dancing. You and your husband are quite a team."

She laughed, "No, honey. That's not my husband." As we went through the door to the dance room, she pointed to a table where another couple sat, "He's her husband. Mine's the gent sitting next to her. We have never danced together since the day we married. He knows how important it is for me to kick up my heels, so I dance with his friend. He takes pleasure in seeing my pleasure."

This was what worked for them. I had to seek my **own** partner. But I wasn't going to be seeking perfection then, just individual moments. For that time, the means was as important as the end. I would enjoy each day. The rest would come.

God had his plan for me, like the song based on the Bible verse, "Turn, Turn, Turn." There is a season for everything under the sun.

Now that I was back in Southern California, I wanted to return to the comfort of my old church. My children and I had always gone there to pray. Even though I was divorced, Catholicism was still my faith, a legacy of religion received and passed to my children. I am a Catholic because I was born to Catholic parents and raised in the church. It is no different from being born into a royal family—you are always part of it. As God is fair and just, I don't think he cares what vehicle we use to get to heaven. So I am a

Catholic, and that comes with guilt. This means going to confession at six years old and trying real hard to come up with a sin you've committed, even though you're clueless as to what it means to be a sinner. But if you weren't one, you'd soon be one. I was smacked for using my left hand because the nun thought it was the work of the devil to be left-handed. It seems to me the church always wants us to ask for forgiveness. Does God really punish you for what you don't know? Did I know what was expected of me at eighteen? When I said, "I do," had I been prepared?

I didn't have all the answers, *but I started going back* to my old church. I had come full circle. Twenty-plus years later I was back where I had skipped the chapter on marriage, had learned to braid my hair looking at the back of Nicole's head, and where some of my children had their first communion. I was coming home.

There was a new building next to what was once the old church. It was beautiful, approximately ten times larger than the old, but the ocean view remained the same. The *new* pastor had hair to his shoulders. After going to Mass for months, I saw he never *once* looked me in the eye as he stood outside the church greeting those who attended mass. I realized that the one constant in my life was my love for God. In that church I saw faces I had known when we used to attend as a family. Though some had embraced me warmly after my long absence, there were those who looked at me as the woman who had once just picked up and left with her children. The *shame* of it. (At least I left *with* my children; I didn't leave them behind.)

It didn't deter me from going, but I felt the pastor needed to know how unwelcoming his attitude had been. I called and made an appointment to see him. It took several phone calls and, in the meantime, I found out about the news the doctor had for me, and I was living alone.

When I finally met with the priest, I told him briefly how this had been my church long ago and how he made me feel unwelcome. His response was that he had often been accused of being detached, and "I'll pray for you." *Pray for me?* There was no explanation for his rudeness, no mention of the fact that I was sitting there, *sweating*, bald, and troubled, in need of assurance.

Later, I heard he had abused a sixteen-year-old girl and paid for her abortion.

Forgive me, Father, for I have sinned.

It reminded me that years before when I was in the hospital because of an accident, Father Mike came to visit. I thought he came to pray with me. Instead, he brought a copy of *The Thornbirds*, a novel about a priest who has an affair. "Read it," he said, thrusting it into my hand. *Later, he was ousted for abuse of young men.*

Forgive me, Father, for I have sinned.

But on the other hand, there are others, so different from these.

One day when I was talking with Father Cavanaugh, who had been a priest for almost sixty years, I asked him, "What would you have done differently if you could do it all over again?"

He had a faraway look in his eyes and said wistfully, "Well, my dear lass, I would never have let Molly McGuire get away from me. But you know, in those days, you did what they told you, and back in Ireland, it was even more so. I did go back and look for her, but she had died some years before." He paused, remembering, and then assured himself, as well as me, "Yes, I would have married Molly McGuire. It gets lonely being a priest. You say the Mass, you hear confession, you tend the sick, but you go home alone. And alone is but alone."

Father Cavanaugh, at eighty-three years old, had spoken his truth. How can you not love a man who speaks the truth? In the past the church, as a wealthy, powerful family, put in the celibacy requirement to make sure money stayed in the family. They didn't want to share it with descendants of priests. It seems that often people or institutions that become powerful abuse their power. I had been told to ask for forgiveness my whole life. Now it seemed it was time that we were asked to forgive.

Despite this, I continued to go to church, because I didn't go to see the priests. I went to be close to God. I needed Him for my life, and though I didn't know it, that life was about to continue a parade of changes.

❋ ❋ ❋

VII.

Take Two:
Look Homeward, Angel

Lunch in Sedona

I always carried inside the dream of a happy marriage, and when I thought once again that I had found it, I gave in to the idea. It lasted briefly, and I usually say I've only been married twice, because I've heard you get to throw one away.

While I learned in my dating experiments that the journey is often more exciting than the destination, any traveler will tell you that one eventually grows weary of the road and longs for home. That's what I thought I had found in Jack.

Jack Van Dan was Dutch and hailed from the same hometown as my grandparents. There was something about him that reminded me of the life I often missed as a teenager in a new country.

He was a kind man, with a round face and receding hairline, but there was a comfort and familiarity about him that drew me in. Maybe it was Dutch cookies on his coffee table or the sound of his mother's voice. She still lived in Holland and reminded me of my grandmother when we talked by phone. My own mother lay dying of a brain tumor, and I felt vulnerable, needing familiarity. His being Dutch brought back so much of what I had been missing. When I was with Jack, I felt I could unpack, put on my favorite slippers, and be who he wanted me to be. Each of us just pretending to be ourselves worked before we married, but so often we play at being someone else to please the one we're with. We accommodate, in order to please. But how long one can play the charade depends on the people involved. We shared a common background, education and culture. I knew my mother would be pleased at my choice because as she lay there in the hospital, she said to me, "Why don't you marry him, then we don't have to worry about you anymore?" Yet all the years before, she would often tell me that if she had it to do all over again, she would really reconsider ever getting married. So I settled in, relieved for the respite. However, before long, I realized a home with Jack was not a home for me. My free spirit conflicted with his need to accumulate wealth. Monetary values were always on his mind. Even if we went to a McDonald's restaurant, he would be talking about how many hamburgers Ray Kroc, owner and founder, had sold that day and how much money that represented. My independence was at odds with his, well, his own idea of independence. We butted heads at every turn, like two stars fighting over who gets the bigger trailer. I found his friends boring; he found mine crazy. My resistance to losing myself led me to finding myself.

Instead of being rejuvenated by my return to my roots, I found that the old adage is true. You can't go home again. I had traveled too far to go back. I was not the young girl fresh off the boat. I needed to find my own home and to accept the fact that sometimes, in life, we must travel alone.

Dancing With Myself

People who stay in long, satisfying marriages continue to fascinate me. I would often ask those lucky enough to be in a happy marriage what they attributed their success to. To succeed in one was the one challenge in life I had yet to conquer, and I was fully aware of my shortcomings in that arena. At this time, I no longer felt envious of the successful couples but more and more began to wonder what made them stay together.

Twice I thought I had what it took, and twice I found out I was wrong.

I came to view marriage as a calling like that of a ballerina. One must have discipline, passion, and that God-given talent to succeed. If there was to be a man in my life, the one common bond I would seek is that we share faith. I trusted God in all things, and I knew that with Him, I was never truly alone. I didn't need anyone to complete me: I was wholly my own person.

When I was not looking, love arrived in the most beautiful way. Before its arrival, however, there were special surprises, and I discovered painting.

❋   ❋   ❋

VII. B

And Beyond:
Mama Wants to Dance

Market Day in Gordes

In the midst of the sadness of my mother's illness and the hopefulness that this was love, there was bright light, closeness with Mama that had never been possible before.

They had been giving her morphine and told us it would be a matter of days. I looked at her, so frail in the bed, and wondered if her life had been all she had hoped for. I prayed that it had. She would smile every time my children came to visit her at the hospital, which was often. I never asked them to; they came on their own, driving over two hours to spend time with their Nanny. They loved her so and had seen a side of her I had only glimpsed at times. They would sit on the bed with her, and she'd wink at them every time a nurse would come to check on her. She would wink with a twinkle in her eye.

Suddenly, she was not my mother, but a young girl again, waiting patiently for the calling that would take her to my sister and all her loved ones who had gone before. There was a peace about her. The look that I used to see in her and in so many other women was gone. Only joy was in her eyes now.

"Moni," she said to me, "sometimes I wish you would just get in the bed with me and stay the whole day."

"You do, Mama?" I asked in surprise.

"The whole day, so we can talk, talk about everything."

"I'd like that, too."

"You know," she whispered, "my sister and I used to be real popular with the boys. Everybody in Castricum knew the Kehl girls. Every Friday night we would go to the café. There would be a band, and we'd dance. I used to dance all night. I used to love to dance," she confided and continued. "Yes, I loved it. One day I saw your father. He was a soldier and came in with a group of guys from Haarlem. You know, that's a big city, and I was just a country girl. Your father was the handsomest man I had ever seen. I could not believe he asked me instead of my sister who was so much more beautiful. So I danced with him, and we got married. But after that, we didn't dance very much anymore. And later he told me he had really been attracted to my older sister, but she already had a boyfriend."

I did want to jump on the bed with her, wanted to hear more. I just looked at her, as she was dozing off, remembering, when suddenly she opened her eyes and, looking nowhere in particular, mumbled to herself, "Just go buy that dress. It has to be green. Just go buy the dress."

"What dress, Mama?" I asked.

"The green dress, the green dress to match my eyes. I want a green dress to match my eyes." I had to strain to hear her.

"Mama, why do you want a dress?" I asked softly.

"Oh, I want a pretty green dress to match my eyes, so I can go dancing with Moni. She loves to dance just like I do." She closed her eyes, and I kissed her forehead, promising we shall dance when we meet again.

VIII.

Art Discovers Me

Gardening Day

I always worked in a variety of ways, from sewing for boutiques in the '70s, to working in restaurants and flower shops, having a gardening business, to modeling. My résumé was infinite. I even tried real estate, but it was not a compatible match. I locked myself in the gate of a courtyard, finally having to climb over a very high block wall in my silk dress and heels. Then when I tried to unlock the door of a condominium, I realized I was in the wrong building. I thought maybe I should think about doing something else.

Later one Friday, as my friend and associate, Gib, and I drove around for the weekly caravan of viewing new listings, I watched all the ladies and gentlemen getting out of their Mercedeses and late-model cars, with their neatly coiffed hairdos, to start the tour. I looked at them and turned to Gib, who was seventy years old and had been in the business for years, and confided, "If that's me in twenty years, I will shoot myself."

He laughed as he looked at me dressed in black jeans and a t-shirt and said, "Yes, that's not you." I soon quit.

Then, when I wasn't looking for a new way to earn a living, it found me. I was just walking down a street in Newport, when my hand started itching. It had often itched since the nuns in the Catholic school in Holland used to hit it with a ruler to make me change to my right hand. This time the itch was more pronounced, and I scratched. I looked to see where I was at the moment of the itching. I was near an artist's paint store I had passed before, but this time I felt myself drawn inside. I looked around the lady's place and admired her work. She told me she gave classes. Why not? It would be a new experience, and I was ready.

In the first class, I saw that Marilyn, the teacher, was a godsend. With her soft-spoken manner, she inspired the students and put them at ease. I later observed that she gave them confidence they needed for their lives in general.

I took just a few classes. When I first picked up a brush, instinctively with my left hand, and saw my paint give life to the canvas, I was hooked. Tears rolled down my cheeks, as I realized I had found what I was meant to do. This was the answer to what had been missing from my whole life. I put on my sunglasses, and beneath them, the tears kept falling. I was at home in this private world between the canvas and me.

For the first assignment, we were to copy another artist. I copied Duane Ault, an Impressionist who spent time in France. I painted his painting of a little boy, which later became a painting of my grandson. I loved doing it. My body felt a warm joy as the colors blended to take a new form. Using my left hand was not the work of the devil as the nuns had said. It was my natural gift.

From that day on, I knew that I was going to paint. After the copied painting, I tried my hand at an original work. From memory, I painted children I had seen sitting on a long pole at a Santa Monica pier. They were five little girls of all races, all laughing together, and two sharing an ice cream cone. There was only one facing the other way, a boy, as if saying, girls are stupid. What went through my mind was that we see girls of diverse backgrounds, just being little girls. The boy didn't want to sit facing the same way with them, not because of ethnicity, just sexism. I loved the scene. The only segregation that came naturally for them was of the sexes. I painted it in a childlike way.

I took the painting to the class. It was still in my car trunk. When I opened the trunk, Marilyn saw it and exclaimed, "Monica, I've had hundreds of students go through my class. Do you know how seldom it is that I find a student with her own recognizable style? *You have style,* and I know one day, you're going to be important. You can come by and paint with me anytime, but I don't want you to change your style." I thanked her, because I knew the other students did try to paint like her. I wasn't going to need classes. I would just paint. I thank Marilyn for seeing that. Rather than trying to have me conform to someone else's style, she gave me the courage to accept my own. From her I learned I can paint what I see, not necessarily what's there. I don't need to sketch first; I can go straight from paint to canvas with acrylics or oils.

Then as I painted, I realized happily that not only did I love painting, but others also admired my work. I created because I wanted to, because I couldn't *not* paint, but it was an extra bonus that others took pleasure from seeing the work. I sold the painting of the children, which I had titled *Peers on the Pier,* to a pediatrician for his office. Later, it was made into tapestries. I took a painting to a framer, and he offered to buy it for $1,200. The next painting I sold to a friend, who bought it in installments. I thought to myself, *Hey, I can do this everyday. I'll open a gallery.* Certainly I'm not cut out for real estate, but I *can* paint.

So by April 3, months after my first art class, I did. I had a building I was leasing, and the tenant left. I thought that it was the right time. I wouldn't try for another tenant; it would become my gallery. It was in an area of Laguna Beach with some elite galleries. I didn't care to compare my work, and I didn't give a rat's ass what anyone thought about it.

I put out my work and waited. One day, two days, and on the tenth day my first painting sold for $400. My daughter and I were thrilled. It took another few days before I sold another one, and in the meantime, I bought a front cover of a local magazine to show my work. This brought many interested lookers, and even some buyers. Over time I started selling many paintings, but it wasn't predictable. There were many days right before the rent was due that I would be sweating it. Sometimes, I'd rent out my house in the summer months and just sleep in the gallery. There were mornings when I would take the garden hose out back of the gallery and shower with cold water. I'd even hand-wash my panties and hang them on the corner of a canvas to dry. One day a man came to me with the panties in hand and asked if they were part of the artwork. I'd forgotten to take them down.

I spent every extra cent I had on advertising and giving my work exposure. I would stay open late at night to possibly attract a nighttime shopper. My daughters helped, which gave me an extra boost. We were even on the *Leeza Gibbons Show*, on a segment titled, "Mothers and Daughters Who Work Together." Leeza held up one of my paintings on the show, and after that even more curious people came by the gallery. Then I appeared on the Phil Donahue show after the *Playboy* issue came out, and again my art and the gallery had exposure. I did other talk shows about women in their forties who were accomplishing their dreams, just "doing it." All of these *events* brought people to the gallery.

Some just came to talk or view the works, like it were a museum, but some came to see and bought works. I hosted many other artists and held exhibitions for Polish-American artists living in California. One exhibit was broadcast by satellite in Poland which brought even more publicity to my Pacific Coast Highway gallery. As a result, I was ***commissioned*** to paint a work of art for the Laguna Beach Film Festival. After that, my work was on posters and t-shirts sold at the festival.

With all of these events, visitors flocked to see my art, and sales were incredible. When I had a successful month, I'd donate a painting to a charity, in appreciation of all my blessings.

It was never really a struggle because my wants were few. Doing what I loved was my reward. The monetary aspect for me was that I was able to afford to do what I loved doing, what I cared about. When we had a good month, I would rent a limo and take my kids and friends to plays. (Night blindness prevented my driving at night.) We'd also go to art openings in Los Angeles. My reward was the work itself. The difficult part was telling someone what a painting cost. I would have liked to have given them all away, but there was rent to pay. I wore my brother's old jeans and often ate at the neighbor's places, so my needs were small. I could just concentrate on enjoying my art. I loved my life.

I enjoyed the gallery and the people who came in to watch me, sometimes to buy, and always to talk. Women would sit around while I painted, at times sharing their dreams with me. Oftentimes I would answer questions about how I had the confidence to just open a gallery, and do what I love to do. Women would confide that they felt stifled, and could only dream of doing what I was doing. Often I'd question them as to why they weren't feeling so dissatisfied and unfulfilled They would share how their lifes had come to a crashing halt once married and after the children came, there had not been time to pick up a paint brush, read a book for pleasure. It all just stopped. Some of the women were sad, and would look longingly at the life of a woman seemingly living her dream. Sometimes I'd tell them there had been many nights of sleeping in the gallery, hoping my neighbors would invite me over for dinner. I would tell them that sometimes one had to give up all the comfort they once knew to follow a dream. It was all about just doing it, and not being afraid to fail. Some walked out uplifted, and many returned.. One woman knelt down in front of one of my paintings and started sobbing uncontrollably, and after a few moments with tears in her eyes, asked if she could just come and visit now and then, to get inspiration. At times I'd fix tea for those who wanted to come and chat with me, sitting in the back room where I painted while keeping an eye on the gallery, talking art, love, children, travel and just being. It was more than just a gallery; it was a place of music, laughter and sometimes tears, a place where a small child was encouraged to pick up a paint brush (with a concerned parent looking on) and encouraged by me to help paint on a canvas I was putting the final brush stroke to. I was at peace, in an environment I created. Always, I had created with God, who inspires me to in all my work. Slowly, the work was recognized by more than those who came to watch or buy. Newspaper writers came to observe and wrote about me in the **LA Times** and in local magazines. The articles often brought welcome mail:

Hi Mo,

This is a long-overdue thank-you note. I was in need of inspiration a few years back when I read your article in Accent. I decided to get off my ass and really *do* something with my life. Last year I graduated from Golden West College. Since February of this year I've participated in several group shows as well as in 3 solo shows, one of which is running now.

I hope you recognize me from past receptions, and yes, I was checking you out. You have an elegant style accompanied by nice moves! I'm sure our paths will cross again in the art world. If you'd ever like a personal tour of Long Beach's "East Village Arts District," I'm the guy. I hope my note finds you well.

T. P. Mullin

❊ ❊ ❊

Dear M. Mo Van:

Just a brief note to thank you for sharing your thoughts. Perhaps, even if we never speak to one another again, our paths were meant to cross in some cosmic nexus, some bizarre crossroads of a simple exchange.

Roger

❊ ❊ ❊

In the articles, my style was described as impressionistic and somewhat primitive with a European ambiance, which

93

inspired lightheartedness in viewers. However they interpreted it, for me, it was about passing fun on to the viewers. I don't worry about making mistakes; I paint from the heart. It's like dancing; there's no right or wrong way, it's about feeling the music. I feel the colors and textures. My paintings come from memories and photographs, anything that touches me. Sometimes an image comes to me on my daily running in the morning, and I'm anxious to get back to put it on a canvas. I like to inspire others to tackle whatever they are doing with an enthusiasm for the task itself, from polishing a table, to singing as you bathe a baby, from cooking a nourishing meal to arranging flowers. It all adds beauty to the world.

After a while, the gallery took on a life of its own. It expanded rapidly. Before long, I eliminated the AND COMPANY from the name. My daughter, Andrea, took over running the gallery when I couldn't be there. We began to sell accessories, which other artists provided, including fabric-covered floral lamps and pillows, ceramics, and wood designs, all in the warm, whimsical setting of the gallery.

In addition to reporters and would-be artists, people who just passed in the night and looked in admired my work. One of them was Ann.

All I knew about her was that *was* her first name. Perhaps she had been asked to leave a residence in the distant past, eons ago. Maybe it was being demolished or made into a condo, and she had no means to find another, nor to find work. Now she slept on a bench by the beach, rain or shine. She spent her days pushing around a grocery cart with her belongings as if she had a destination. Often she would stop and stare in the window of the gallery, perhaps to see the art, perhaps to catch a glimpse of herself. Sometimes she'd offer suggestions on how better to display the paintings. I listened and once in a while I'd make a change, just to see her smile. One day she passed dressed in fine linens, navy blue slacks and a white shirt. She peered in the door and called out to me, "Mo Van, where are you? Hey, Mo Van."

Café de France

I walked to the front of the gallery and saw her weather-beaten face, hair gray at the roots, bleached by the sun, smiling as if in all her sixty-plus years she had done something she remembered well. Oh, what a face. It was burdened by years of living outside, without the benefit of sunscreen or hat. The deep crevices in her face reminded me of a canvas, an abstract painting. Interesting. Where were her children? Had her mother held her, read books to her, walked her to school? Had she herself ever answered to the word "Mama"? Was there a place she had called home in another lifetime? Lying on her bench, listening to the sound of the ocean, did she ever recall a familiar song or two? Did she for a moment remember getting into bed knowing a man was waiting for her with anticipation? Had her body smelled of perfume? Had she danced and listened to the words of a particular song and thought it was forever? Could she still smell the scent of the after-shave he wore, and had he ever made her blush? I wanted to ask but didn't. Today, in her linens, she held a Styrofoam cup in her hand, wanting to chat.

"I stood in front of the gallery last night, and you know I felt your paintings. I mean I was on that little street with the bright umbrellas. I sat at that table." She pointed to the bistro table in a painting of Café de France. "I could hear Edith Piaf sing. You know, Mo Van, I've never been to France, but I was there last night, sipping fine red wine. And I wasn't pushing no shopping cart. Thank you for such 'happy paintings.'"

"Ann, you look great in your linens. Maybe I should be doing what you are doing. Look at me in my torn jeans, T-shirt full of paint, and you look as if you just came from a fashion show. What's wrong with this picture?"

"Oh, Mo Van, I had a *good* day yesterday. I walked past the Goodwill truck, and you know, these were lying on top of the bag, so I just took them. Don't think it's stealing, since I'm one of, as they say, the less fortunate ones. And look, they fit. I was going to save them for a special occasion, but I thought, visiting you today was special enough. You think God will think of it as stealing?"

"Are you kidding? There is a reason you are looking like you just walked out of *Vogue*. Someone wanted you to look elegant today." I hugged her and smelled the street, the booze, and cigarette smoke of someone who bathed in sinks at gas stations, slept on park benches. I smelled a woman who would sometimes walk to Fashion Island and spend the day at the cosmetic counter, having make-up applied to her face, taking the samples with her, *but more in need of human touch*.

Standing there, she shook her cup, as if asking for a refill. She wanted more coffee, something to eat. She didn't say the words. They usually don't. She looked past me into the gallery and murmured, "I'd best be on my way. I have a lot to do." She turned the cup upside down, emphasizing its emptiness.

I reached in my back pocket and handed her a twenty-dollar bill. It was Friday, a day of promise for a beautiful weekend, and in that moment I was her, and she was I, and we were two beings standing in the doorway of life.

"Oh, Mo Van. That's just too much. You've given me way too much. It's just too much." She had a bewildered look on her face, almost frightened. I took the twenty out of her hand and, agreeing with her, replaced it with a ten. She looked down and smiled, thanking me all the while. She hugged me again and told me, "I best be going now." I watched her as she pushed her cart up the street, looking back, waving, as she distanced herself from me. Her not wanting to accept the twenty, but being more elated with the ten, might explain her pushing a cart.

So, from those looking, to those coming in to stay awhile, the pleasure of the gallery was the people and their reactions. I heard people say, "I look at your paintings, and I'm happier."

"I look at your paintings, and I hear music."

"I see your paintings, and I wish I were there." Just hearing that once or twice in a lifetime is sweet enough.

And I like the children's views. Once a child asked, "Why don't you put faces on the people in your paintings?" His mother nearly fainted that he had even had a question about the painting.

I answered him with a question of my own, "Why do you think I don't put faces?"

He thought a moment and came up with, "If you put a face on it, you'd have to look at the same face every day. But not putting a face, you can put any face you want on it." Children often see beyond the vision of adults. His parents thanked me for the visit, gave me a hug, and promised they'd be back. I just smiled. The young feel my ideas of art internally.

ART and OTHER CREATIVITY

IT IS NOT IN THE KNOWING, BUT IN THE DOING. *******
THERE IS NO SUCH THING AS PERFECTION. PERFECTION LIES IN
HOW WE HANDLE IMPERFECTIONS. ******
CRITICS OF THE ARTS ARE MURDERERS. *******
SHOW ME A CRITIC, AND I'LL SHOW YOU SOMEONE WHO HAS
NEVER CREATED. ***********

IF FEAR OF NOT BEING PERFECT KEEPS US FROM DOING, WE'LL
NEVER DO ANYTHING. SO, GO OUT AND DO. YOU CAN.

❁   ❁   ❁

Children inspire my photographs and memories, but my
parents who taught me to value and enjoy working also
inspire me. My papa never actually recognized me as a
painter. He would watch me paint when I would go out to
look after him in his home, but if people asked what I did,
he couldn't bring himself to say, "She's an artist." He had
been to *the* gallery, walking around, taking it all in. He
never asked if I had sold any paintings. What he would say
was, "Did you dance today?" This was because I used to
dance for joy when I made a sale. I'd dance with whichever
daughter was working in the gallery with me that day.

Then I had my first show. It was in Newport Beach at
an upscale Italian restaurant, Saporis. I was excited as I sold
one painting after another, seventeen out of twenty, plus
ceramics and tapestries with my design. It had been a great
success, and I couldn't wait to tell Papa. Maybe now, he
would acknowledge his daughter, if not for having talent,
for at least having the guts to paint.

The phone rang toward the end of the show. It was my
brother who told me, "Hurry home." I left immediately and
started the two-hour drive to Papa's home.

As I drove, I hoped he was all right and I realized I was
so thankful that I had come to know him, not only as a
father, but a friend. When I was young, he seemed in the
background, as a disciplinarian. He never asked how a party
was or if we had a part in the school play. Even my friends,
years later, told me they were afraid of him, of his stern look.

It was the birds that brought out his softer side. He could be completely himself with them. He would go out to the patio, whistling softly so as not to disturb them and put out food and water. He was equally at home with flowers, growing lilies he showed me with the hint of a smile, lilies he put by Mama's picture in the living room. We'd sit by the lilies in the patio and actually talk. This was something I always wanted with my mother, but except for that day at the hospital, we never had the chance. He would tell stories about being young, going to war, working in New Guinea. He talked about the operas he liked on KCET. He also confided, "During the war, my buddy and I were in Poland and he went to see a prostitute and found she had a bottle of Vodka in her money drawer. I had to go see her, too." I frowned to myself, not sure if I wanted to hear the rest of the story, but he added mischievously, "Not to be with her, but to get the Vodka. I would never have paid for sex, ever. No one had alcohol during the war. *I was just thirsty, you know what I mean.*" We shared laughter.

As I made the drive up from the coast toward his home, wishing it were shorter, I remember all the days I was taking him to lunch, grocery shopping for him, talking and listening, but mostly laughing. I never would have thought the strict father I knew in Holland was full of so much fun. He had even stopped me one night as I was leaving, and put his arm on my shoulder to say, "You know I love you, don't you?" I didn't know what to say. I had never heard him say those words before.

The only reply I could think of was, "It took you long enough." I was forty at the time. Forty years to hear the words, although he must have thought he expressed his love by caring for us all, never having been heard to complain, and always singing or whistling on his way to and from work, contrary to his disposition at home. I had needed to hear the words from him. That night I had driven around over eleven hours, replaying the sweetness of those words that came so late.

As much as I enjoyed hearing those words, I also wanted to hear him say he **liked** my art, to validate me as an artist. So many others had, but he was my father. I once painted a Dutch landscape scene with windmills and a cottage surrounded by flowers. He said it made **him** feel good to look at it, and he asked if I would hang it where he could see it from his recliner. He could look into it, into his childhood home. That in itself was a compliment, not really saying I was an artist, but saying my art made him feel good. Some words, for some reason, just couldn't come out, though they were surely there. Later, he even said, forgetting that I had painted the picture, "Be sure, when I'm gone, you and your brother don't fight over this. Be sure your brother puts it in his home." I agreed, taking this as another indirect compliment.

It was special to me because he had watched me paint it, commenting on the usage of color and the objects. It was just those actual words of calling me a painter that I longed to hear, now as I was getting closer to his house, with the news of all the sales I had made. Maybe tonight he would see I was a **professional** artist and say something.

It wasn't to be. As I pulled into the driveway, the nurse was motioning for me to rush in. I ran up the steps and into his room. When I took my father's hand, I made the sign of the cross on his forehead and whispered the "Our Father."

Then I watched him slip away. I never could tell him about the show or the many paintings I sold. It was too late. There was no more, but we had those moments. It was my painting he had wanted to see from his recliner. We had the feeding of the birds, the storytelling, *listening to K.D. Lang*, the gathering of fresh flowers to put next to Mama's photo, harmonizing in the kitchen, while he proudly did the cooking for this daughter who came to visit on a weekly basis. Those moments are mine to cherish.

And there were to be other connections, communications. . . .

PLEASE COME BACK

It was a beautiful Saturday afternoon, and I could see the Pacific Ocean from my back window. Andrea Bocelli was singing "Con Tu Partiro." Paintbrush in hand, I was putting the finishing touches to a new work on my canvas. The gallery was located on Pacific Coast Highway, between Wahoes Fish Tacos and the Toporowicz Gallery. As I sat there painting and singing along with Andrea, a woman walked in and stood behind me for several minutes, observing. She took a piece of fabric out of her purse and excitedly announced that this was the painting she had been looking for. Although it was not yet completed, she wanted to buy it. I turned to look at her and introduced myself. I was somewhat in disbelief because earlier in the day, I had already sold four other paintings. I couldn't believe my ears when she casually insisted that this one was it, the object of her long search. It wasn't everyday that I sold a painting, but that day I was having incredible luck—four already sold, and another, not yet completed, being bought.

As we exchanged pleasantries and made arrangements for her to pick up her painting the following week, a bird flew into the gallery. It came toward the back and landed on the stool, which held my paintbrushes and solvent. It flew back to where my painting hung, and, as if viewing the paintings, came back and flew out of the door. "Oh, that must be my father," I said calmly.

The lady looked at me questioningly, as if wondering if she heard correctly. I continued, "Yes, I am sure that was Papa. I just wish I had my camera when he landed on that stool, so I could have taken his picture."

No sooner had I said the words than the bird flew back and landed on the stool. I grabbed my camera and snapped a photo, with only one picture left. He flew back out. I knew, finally, that my father had acknowledged me as an artist. He had told me before he died, "You will see me in many things."

I knew.

There were more visits. . . .

※　※　※

HAPPY BIRTHDAY, PAPA

My sister, Marjan, and I were talking on the morning of July 1, which would have been my father's eighty-first birthday. In Holland the birthday song goes something like, "Long shall he live in the glory." We broke into that song, honoring our father on the day of his birth, as we believed he was now in the glory of God. We spoke on the telephone for some time and reminisced about days gone by, as sisters will do. I told her how I saw our parents in many things—sometimes a bird, sometimes a rose, or in a song. He loved the sound of K.D. Lang, and when I heard her sing, the thought of him would come to mind.

On this morning I was sharing with my sister how I missed both our parents, and it seemed the older I became, the more I realized how much they had sacrificed for us. The conversation continued for some time, and although we both wished our childhood years could have been more pleasant, we acknowledged that our parents had done their best and certainly not without challenges. Yes, now as a grown woman I could say that maybe they hadn't been ideal parents, but they had been incredible human beings. In the long run, that was more important to me as a grown-up child. My sister and I hung up, and I hurriedly dressed to go to my gallery. I decided to give the day in honor of Papa.

Entering the gallery, I walked to the back and played my phone messages. An unfamiliar female voice spoke, "Good morning, Mo Van. It is eight a.m. and I'm standing in front of your window, looking at your paintings. I don't know you, but I thought you would want to know that while I was admiring your work, a bird suddenly landed on the easel facing the street. I thought you might want to check to see if you can find it when you open the gallery this morning." I played and replayed the message many times. I called my sister and had her listen, remembering that at 8:00 a.m., we were singing together for our papa. I looked around the gallery, and I found a white feather underneath my latest painting—a painting of a landscape of Holland with a windmill in the background. I picked up the feather and held it close. Again, I knew.

❀ ❀ ❀

THE DUTCH BAKER

Beyond visits from my father, there were other special happenings.

Often, in years past, I would stop at the Holland American store in Artesia on the way to Papa's house. Mama had been gone for some time, and he would love it when I would bring him cookies, drop (licorice) and sometimes even frozen fresh herring. The Polish love their pieroges bought at a Delekateski, and the Germans love their sausage. Nothing makes one feel more at home than the taste and sight of traditional foods from one's homeland. However, because the Holland American store was located an hour or so from my house, and the memories of going there always reminded me of the last years Papa and I had shared, really getting to know each other, the thought of going there, knowing he was no longer here, was really difficult.

I stopped going for several years until, two weeks before one Christmas, I realized that maybe it would be a good idea to send off some Dutch treats to my aunt living in Tahoe, and send surprise packages to my children. The children, having taken a liking to Dutch licorice, cookies, and other treats, had more than once asked when I could go to the

Dutch store again. For some time I pondered going as it was getting closer to Christmas. I kept postponing the trip.

Then one Friday morning I decided that once I got back from my walk up the hill I would have arrived at my decision. It was either to go that day, or not go at all. I walked up the hill, and when I reached the top, a van pulled up across the street. An elderly man got out and smiled as he greeted me. "Hello, Monica," he said. "What are you doing all the way up here?" I was sweaty, and I told him how I try to walk up the hill every morning before going to the gallery.

"Better yet," I said. "how about you, isn't this out of your way"?

"Well, you know, my son lives right there, and we are going to a funeral, so I am here to pick him up."

I walked closer to him. "Okay, but why do you have such a big van?"

He smiled and said, "I am the Dutch Baker." He pulled open the double doors, and started pulling out deep drawers filled with everything I had imagined: cookies, cakes, licorice, cold cuts kept in the refrigerated part of the van.

"You are an angel," I told him.

Since Dutch people are rather blasé, he just looked at me in that funny sort of way as if to say, I don't know what she is talking about. I started grabbing everything I wanted to buy, and after he totaled it, and put it in bags for me, I realized I did not have any money. I promised to send him a check as soon as I got home. He just smiled.

Walking down the hill with my arms full of Dutch goodies, I had never felt my father's presence as I did that very moment. I knew I had just experienced a Christmas miracle.

I sent my angel a check in the amount of $98.12, a package to my aunt and on to my children. A few days later my cousin called and said my aunt was watching Miracle on 34th Street. She was a little sad, thinking of all the Christmases of so long ago, when her husband, my uncle, was still alive, and my parents and all of us would be together. She was longing for all the goodies the Dutch Baker would bring, a longing inspired by that little girl sitting on Santa's lap in the miracle story, who was singing a Dutch Christmas song, "Sinter Klaas Kapoentje," when the UPS man knocked on the door with a box full of everything she could imagine from the Holland American store. She cried to the deliveryman, "It's a miracle!"

IX.

Hitting a Bump

Arches

Life was flowing smoothly like a mountain stream, with bright flowers along the bank. I was enjoying my children, grandchildren, friends, and art, with true love still off-stage, until a bolt of lightning struck. Before that, I was savoring the ride.

The gallery next door had parties, and I joined them after painting all day. There were always people from Russia, Romania, France, Poland—all dancing to Felini's music, conversing in a surreal atmosphere of paintings hanging from chains around us in a half-lit room with plenty of garlic-flavored stuff to eat. The owner and I were two foreign artists making a home in the somewhat pseudo colony of art in the beach city of Laguna. For many years I had so much. I spent time with the owner of the gallery next door, cooking and enjoying our visitors. Coffee, tea, wine, vodka and conversation abounded, in a life that couldn't last, but I savored it while it did.

Once in a while, I would stop on the way home and dance alone in a gay bar on Pacific Coast Highway. Men danced with men, and I could just feel the music and spin around alone on the wooden floor, energized, before going home. It was just the fun of dancing, without thoughts of making conversation.

At this time I was enjoying the colors and music of a magical life. I had my gallery and the one next door to dance in. Some other time, some other place, I would dance with a caring man, in the harmony of love.

Meanwhile, at the parties in the gallery next door and in my own, I was meeting people. They came to my place to admire my work, critique, or a few, just to get out of the rain. In the neighboring gallery, a Polish couple was discussing my art in a mocking manner, not knowing I was the artist. The wife declared, "I see paintings next door. They are perfect for kitchens and bathrooms."

I laughed. "Thank you," I answered. "I'm glad there are so many kitchens and bathrooms in the world." *Her husband displayed his work nearby, and though he was a highly trained artist, his work rarely sold.* Visitors, local and people from around the world liked the honesty of my work; they said that it *"evoked a feeling" in them that they enjoyed.* They were simply *happy scenes.*

Another artist I met at this time was Johan, a prestigious, well-schooled painter who came here from Romania. He became my mentor and friend, and I valued his opinion. His seriousness contrasted with my flamboyance, and he taught me so much. He studied my paintings and one day asked in awe, "How do you get those vivid colors? They're amazing." I couldn't answer. What was *amazing* was someone who was such an incredible artist asking how I painted. Also, I couldn't answer because the work is something you feel inside, which can't be explained to others, even another artist. It was satisfying to hear it from him.

I had finally reached a pinnacle where I didn't have to be in constant struggle. The children were grown, and I was doing the work I adored. I was taking care of myself, so I'd keep this vibrancy, practicing yoga, drinking carrot juice and running every morning on the beach in front of my cottage. Because of this, my daughter sent some pictures of me to *Playboy* magazine for fun. They were celebrating forty years of publishing, and I was forty-five. I was shocked when they called me, but I thought it was a good idea to show how women are beautiful at any age. In other countries, men acknowledge this, seeing more beauty and wisdom in an older woman, like fine wine. In America there is often a devaluation of women as they grow older, while showing a greater respect for men with years. So, wanting to show that vibrancy and being lovely are timeless, I agreed. However, I insisted the photographs be in good taste. They were. In the photo shoot, I have no clothes, but enough is covered, so that I show less than is shown everyday on California beaches, and certainly less than is shown on European beaches. It was nothing that would embarrass my children or grandchild, but just show that the sparkle of life is ageless.

Enjoying this agelessness, I continue to travel the path, taking in the wild flowers along the way. During this time I was seeing the comedian and impersonator, Rich Little, for a while. One day, we were hiking down a mountain in Sedona, Arizona, and upon reaching the bottom of Cathedral Mountain we were stopped by two young girls, who asked him, "Would you please use our camera and take a picture of us together?" He did, but because he was used to people asking for his picture or autograph, this was somewhat humiliating. He had done imitations of presidents and movie stars, performed in front of the queen of England, yet as the young girl handed him her camera he was just someone, nameless and inconsequential. For so many years, he assumed everyone on the planet knew of him. Not unlike the one night we had made reservations for dinner and when we showed up there seemed to be some confusion when he stated his name. The young hostess at the podium asked, "Did you say Lettle?" And for the second time he said, "No, I said Little." The maitre d', looking over her shoulder, read the name out loud and, without looking up, repeated, "Little as in Rich Little," not realizing Rich was standing right in front of him.

I just laughed to myself, knowing that no matter who you may have become, someone doesn't care who you are.

After that, I threw myself a big fiftieth birthday party. I rented a huge house, so all my friends from out of town had a place to stay. Rich's gift to me was a performance for all my family and friends. But more important than his presence was being able to look around the room and seeing all the people I loved, who loved me. It was overwhelming. I had to thank them. I stood up and, taking my time, spoke to each one, recognizing something unique about every one of them. The group included my former sister-in-law and former mother-in-law from my marriage to Jeffrey, Jack van Dam's sister, the aunt and grandmother of my children. I had a special bond with each. Standing there, acknowledging family, ex-family, friends, and other artists, I realized how truly blessed I was to have been able to keep all of them in my life. It felt great seeing my eighty-year-old-plus ex-mother-in-law, sitting, smiling as she fought back tears of joy when I introduced her as "the best mother-in-law one could ask for." Rich was no longer the one star, each person was a star.

I wanted every one to know how important he or she was.

What matters is who you are to yourself. I had all these friends and family around me, but also I was learning to be content being alone, but not lonely. Yet my eyes were always open. Some friends called me Patches because I was like an inner-tube, they said, floating along, hitting a bump, putting on a patch and going on, as good as new, but maybe wiser.

Then I hit *the one* that sent me spinning. Driving home from the gallery one night, I made a turn, and my arm brushed against my breast. Something was there. I froze. It could not *be*. Yet, in a way, I had almost expected it. Though I was eating every healthy food and exercising to ward it off, it came anyway.

At home I showered and did the breast self-exam. There was no longer any doubt. It was a lump. After first facing this reality, my next reaction was to whisper to myself, "Thank goodness it's not one of my *daughters*."

I knew I had to have a biopsy right away, but it was two days before Thanksgiving, and I didn't want to spoil *the* holiday. Also, saying it aloud would give it more validity. I went through the motions of preparing dinner, with the traditional foods and family, trying to be *myself*, but this was not something I could keep to myself long. I did confide in one person, my ex-husband's brother, who had been my friend since high school and was a guest for the feast. At a quiet moment in the kitchen I took his hand and brought it to the outer side of my right breast. "Yeah," I said finally, "you get a quick feel and that is it." He, too, felt the grape-sized lump and silently gave me a brotherly hug. I told him to please guard my confidence. He again hugged me in silence. Now it was out.

It was officially stamped real when I went to the doctor. At first he gave me a mammogram, and then he said, "You're fine. See you next year."

As much as I would have liked it to be true, I knew it wasn't. I had him feel what I felt. He ran a sonogram and called a radiologist, who confirmed my *suspicions*.

115

THEN CAME THOSE TEN DAYS OF WAITING, PRAYING, REFLECTING.

I had my faith and my inner determination. Also, my children were my strength. I don't know how I could have gone through it without their encouragement. I had my time to absorb what was happening in the quiet moments alone, like an earthquake-proof building that rocks with seismic waves but stays standing. I thought of my mother, father, sister, and uncles who all had survived less than a year after their diagnosis. I wept for them as I hadn't before. How many months did I have? I wasn't actually afraid. Once you face the thought of dying and meet it head-on, nothing else can terrify you. You are fortified.

Two hundred and forty hours of waiting have to be lived through. There's no way to speed up the clock. I tried reading the paper, but I couldn't concentrate.

Then **Kristen** came by for a little handholding and empathy, and when she left, I found a letter, just like those I used to find when they were little.

Dear Mom,

It's 4:30 a.m., and I can't sleep. But you know what, Mom, I think of you and all you have gone through since you were 18, and I know, whatever happens, you'll make it. You have to go through the bad to get to the good. You have raised 4 beautiful children, and when we drove you crazy, when you could have just wanted to give up and crawl into a hole and forget about the world, you hung in there. You really have had one of the toughest yet most rewarding jobs. I love you, Mom. Nobody could have ever done such a wonderful job raising 4 children. I don't think we let you know often enough how thankful we are for your raising us as well as you did. You are my inspiration in life and always will be. Whenever I need a shoulder to cry on, you are there. Whenever I need help, you help me. When I think of the times I have hurt or disappointed you, I get so mad at myself. Because you're the last person on this earth I would ever want to hurt. You really have done a lot for me. Sometimes I wish I had never become an adult. Then I would know I would never have to be away from you. I really hope you believe I appreciate all you do for me each day of my life. You are the "bestest" friend anybody could have.

I remember when I was young, and I would come home from school, and I would cry because the kids picked on me. You always told me how special I was and you always made me feel so much better. Mom, I promised I would support you someday, and you never broke a promise to me, and I am not going to break that promise to you, no matter what happens in life. You really taught me a lot. I really hope this letter makes you happy because I mean it all from the bottom of my heart. I LOVE YOU, MOM! You are the best and I thank God for giving me such a wonderful human being for my mom and best friend.

Love, Kristen

❅ ❅ ❅

Well, of the 480 half-hours, this had to be the best, reading and rereading letters sent to me over the years. Taking the time to read the words written at different times from family and friends. It brought it all closer and gave my life clarity. There were still so many more to go. I could bathe, walk, go out to my garden, fix a snack, go for the mail. Go to the box, which held many notes written throughout the years, and pray. In it was a letter in scrawled handwriting from my grandson.

Dear Moni,

Today I am remembering when you danced like a gypsy. You held out your hands and coaxed me, "Come dance with me. Dance with me to the end of love. You clap your hands, with your eyes closed, smiling, watching the gypsies dance deep in your soul. Come dance like a gypsy." You kept saying. I wanted to dance but had no idea what a gypsy was. I was only four at the time, sitting next to your old friend Bill. He knew what a gypsy was. He was the oldest man I had ever known. He was 80 years older than me, and he could see the gypsies, I think. He said they wore big earrings, and their skirts sashayed to the sounds of violins. I then told you that the gypsy lost her earring and you bent down and picked it up, and held it in the palm of your hand before handing it to me. You were just dancing in your chair, and suddenly I knew how a gypsy looked and all I could see were gold earrings, colorful skirts, and beautiful long dark hair. I loved that night listening to Leonard Cohen, watching you dance, and never telling me once to eat my dinner. And even the old man told me that although he had never met a real gypsy he was certain that you had been one in another life. He told me it was a special night. It was Valentine's night. And it was just the three of us, and the gypsy.

P.S. "That's it," I told you. It was Valentine's night, and we had meatballs and spinach, like you used to have in

Holland. You didn't tell me to eat my spinach; you just danced like a gypsy. You, the old man and me. It was a very special night. Do you remember?

Love, Kyle

❀   ❀   ❀

How could I not remember? I had so many special memories, enough for two lifetimes, but I still wanted more. If I had what I feared I might have, I was going to conquer it, and make new ones. The numbers on the digital clock clicked off another minute.

Finally, when the phone did ring, I hesitated to pick it up, but I mustered the strength. This was the call. My friends, Marci and Tony, my neighbors and friends, a couple close to me, hugged me as they saw my face receive the news, "You have breast *cancer*. We need to operate." Preceding the news that now I had been officially diagnosed with what I had feared for so long, all I remember from that startling call was that it had a name, and all the words spoken before "Yes, you have cancer" were immediately forgotten.

Somehow I got to the hospital, with my children there, holding my hand before the surgery. When I awoke, still groggy, I heard, "Everything went great. We got it all out. The lymph nodes are clean." They reassured me, "It hasn't spread."

I breathed a sigh of relief, but only for a few days. The news changed; the nodes were affected. I would need aggressive chemotherapy for seven months, followed by six weeks of radiation. I had to quit my hormone replacement therapy, as I would be taking—and still take—Tamoxefin, which acts adversely with estrogen. There was another scare. After looking at my MRIs, they said the cancer had in probability metastasized to the brain. But after another oncologist reexamined the scans, he suggested I go to a neurologist because there was the possibility that there were signs of multiple sclerosis. I personally took the report and scan to a neurologist, and, while waiting in the waiting room, pulled the report and read there was a possibility that I might be in the early stages of MS. Seeing the words spelled out, my only thought was how I should react if indeed the report turned out to be correct. As I waited, sweating, in that moment, with the challenge of beating cancer ahead of me, with the possibility of being diagnosed with multiple sclerosis, I looked up and said to no one in particular, "If I have to, I can do this, too."

My name was called, and as I entered, Dr. Carroll took my hand in a comforting manner. As he glanced at the scans against the light coming through the window, he put my mind at ease by telling me that although there was ample white scar tissue visible, due to migraine headaches I had suffered for years—and cause for concern to those without expertise in this field—at this point my only concern should be conquering my breast cancer, and, half-jokingly, finding a spouse to share my life with.

I left his office feeling good for the first time in a long time. Now "just" fighting my cancer seemed not nearly as difficult as it did before entering his office.

It could have been worse, had the MS diagnosis been correct. Now it was "only" cancer facing me.

When I was going to go to surgery, I prepared myself. I thought of my mother who had seen the pope on television when he was in the U.S. and then felt at peace to die. I had my moment of peace, but I wanted to prepare my family, so I wrote this letter. It was only to be read if I didn't make it. I held their hands just before I was wheeled into the operating room.

❊ ❊ ❊

Dear Children,

This is just to remind all of you how I'll never be far away from you. Just know that your mother lived her life to the fullest, enjoyed it to the max, and you must always remember me smiling, laughing, and looking forward to playing the game in "Life." And let me tell you, I have really lived It, as you know. Never a good time to say, "Good-bye," and that is why we just say, "So long."

My biggest claim to fame has been having you for my children because no mother could have felt more blessed than I. I'll always remember all the laughter, the disagreements with fondness, and the tears, with joy. Tell me, didn't we have it all? And we always will.

As I'm sitting here thinking about not being here, I must fight the tears, not for me, but for the loss you will feel. That is why I'm writing now. I know how I hurt when my mom left me and there was yet so much to tell her. Well, I want to tell you all, that there is nothing you didn't tell me, for I do know and have always felt the love you had for me. I always felt all the love from all of you. And damn, was I ever lucky. I was blessed, and God was good to me to have allowed me to give life to you.

Love God, for He is good. Do not cry except tears of joy. Do not be angry, for we really had it all, and it will always be with us, until we meet again. You will think of me when you hear Anne Murray sing, ". . . in the morning, when I rise . . ." and too many things to mention now. But you will know, and I will know.

Dudley, oldest son, love and take care of your sisters. Be there for them, like you always have. Laura, stay as beautiful on the inside as you are on the outside. Kristen, I will be there at your opening, because you can do anything you set your mind to. Andrea, I know you know. You are the baby, but the tallest. You are sweet and moody like your mom. Stay close to your family. I'm so proud of you all, and I want you to always remember the "hand." I don't want to sit here and tell you how proud I am and why I love you all so much. You must all know the reasons. This note is just to let you know that someone else may not believe that "No one ever dies." But I say if a soul cannot be operated on, as a heart may be replaceable, or a kidney, lung or other body parts, a soul is ours and as our bodies fail us, our soul keeps going. If you cannot kill it or take it from me, it cannot die. Our souls will stay connected, forever. So play some good music and dance, dance, dance and sing, for I'll be there with you all.

Thanks for being my angels and the bestest kids any mother could have ever hoped for.

Love, Mom

P.S. Throw a party, invite all your friends, and have a ball.

＊　＊　＊

I'm still around, but the sentiments are still a part of me. I never wanted my children to question my love for them, or have them have any doubt about what a great life and kids God had blessed me with. There were many things I could have improved upon in this life, but being a *mother* was the ultimate. And this I never wanted them to doubt.

I woke up to see all my children around me. Whew! I was going to have time for years more of memories to add on. Then there was the war of chemotherapy versus my cancer cells. Going into the chemo room, I was as nervous as hell. I was about to be hooked up to a needle that would drip poisons in my arm for four hours. There were already three men in the room, staring grimly at nothing. One looked already half-gone, and the other two were very old. I took a breath and said lightly, "Lucky me. It's the first time I'm here, and I have three good-looking men with me, and it is only Monday." They all laughed. A drill-sergeant-type nurse stormed in and bellowed, "We'll have to keep it down in here." To which I replied mockingly, "We are not dead yet."

I couldn't believe it. Following her outside, I matched her determination with my own, "Don't you *ever* talk to people like that again." When I went back, one of the old men winked at me, as I was bracing myself for the needle. I survived against chemo, and chemo against the raging cells, but not without some battle scars, nausea, intense sweating and a loss of hair.

At first I used wigs, but they itched. Also, there was dignity in baldness. It could show all who saw me that I overcame cancer, that they need not be afraid. There was a certain nice feeling in being able to rub my head, something I would not have normally known.

I tried to make it a lucky gesture for my grandchildren—rubbing my head would be like rubbing Aladdin's lamp. Each could make a wish. They came into the room and hugged me, so delighted I was the same old Moni, as they called me. The flowers and lit candles everywhere gave the room a mystical look. Then slowly I removed my colorful silk scarf and exposed my head. They gasped inaudibly, but I reassured them, "Come on over and make a wish. Pretend that I am a genie. It's good luck."

Paulo, my grandson, ten at the time, came closer first and touched my head. With tears in his eyes, he made a silent wish, and everything was easier after that. I knew they knew their grownup Moni could die. They just wanted me well again. Then Kyle and Nico came forward. Little four-year-old Kyle touched it and gave a quick, "Your head feels funny. Moni, can we go to the beach now?" He wanted things like they always were. But it was Paolo whose words said it clearly. First he proclaimed, "Don't worry. You're still beautiful and have the prettiest bald head I've ever seen." Then, quieter, he added, "I'm praying that God will make you better, and when your cancer is gone, your hair will be more beautiful than ever." We all looked at each other. He had said the word we had been avoiding, but kids aren't stupid. It was a relief to finally have it out in the open. Talking about it was a step in conquering. They knew what they wanted: their grandmother healthy again. All I wanted was their love. We served tea, chanted, and all held hands. The flowered scarf experience was special.

I had heard of children who had shaved their heads to

make a child with cancer feel part of the group, but I didn't need that. At some point someone in the family said they would all shave their heads if it would make me feel better. My daughters looked at me, startled, gulping. No way did they want to shave their long, beautiful hair. They would have if it would have made me well, but for just an all-in-the-same-boat feeling, please. It was the last thing they wanted to do. They'd have rather ridden nude on white elephants down Rodeo Drive. I laughed to myself and assured them it wasn't necessary. Sighs. Just their presence was always enough.

However, I was determined to show my bald head when I went out, as a symbol that it's all right to be bald, that cancer could be overcome.

We entered the gala event; after all it was an art exhibit, showing Linda McCartney's artworks, benefiting many breast cancer charities. Going sans wig or scarf seemed like a brilliant idea, showing others that there are worse things than not having hair. My girlfriend looked dismayed when I exited my house as she picked me up. She looked questioningly, not unlike the others at the event, who automatically looked away immediately upon seeing a bald woman walk proud. I was proud to be there, proud to pay my respects to an artist and woman who had fought her fight.

Hair grows back. Strong new body cells replace old ones. My skin never looked so good. My hair came in thicker than before. Soon I started comparing my treatments to a beauty overhaul. Often I was asked to talk to others about my treatments, coping skills, and positive attitude, particularly in comparing the treatments to a beauty cure. Thinking of it in that light made it easier for others and me.

125

I was asked to write a story for **Chicken Soup for the Soul**, a breast cancer survivor story, but declined, thinking one day I would write my own version of it all. There is a Bible verse in Corinthians that says, "The foolish of the world shall lead the wise." I felt that I, the foolish, might be able to help the wise.

I continued to go to the *gallery*, although I might feel tired. Art and the people who came to see it refreshed me. One of the *LA Times* reporters who had been there before came back and wrote:

FROM A LOS ANGELES TIMES REPORTER, DAVID:

I'D KNOWN MO VAN FOR AT LEAST A YEAR BEFORE SHE CASUALLY REVEALED THAT, A FEW YEARS AGO, SHE'D BEEN IN PLAYBOY, AS PART OF A PHOTO FEATURE (IS THERE ANY OTHER TYPE?) TITLED SOMETHING LIKE, "WOMEN WE LOVE OVER 40." "IT WAS NO BIG DEAL," SHE SAID, SHRUGGING, AS IF IT WERE THE MOST NATURAL THING IN THE WORLD FOR A WOMAN WHO WAS ALMOST 50 TO APPEAR WITHOUT CLOTHES IN A MAGAZINE. I NEVER SAW THE PICTORIAL. NOT THAT MO VAN WAS AGAINST MY SEEING IT. SHE PROMISED ME EVERY TIME WE AGREED TO HAVE LUNCH THAT SHE'D BRING THE MAGAZINE ALONG. BUT THEN SHE'D SHOW UP WITHOUT IT, AND SHE'D SAY SHE FORGOT. AGAIN, I THINK SHE DIDN'T WANT TO MAKE A BIG DEAL OUT OF BEING A GRANDMOTHER AND AN ICON FOR COLLEGE-AGED (AND OLDER) BOYS. I ALSO THINK THAT SHE DIDN'T WANT ME TO THINK OF HER AS A MO VAN PLAYBOY PLAYMATE. THAT CERTAINLY WASN'T HOW SHE THOUGHT OF HERSELF, AND SINCE I'D KNOWN HER FOR A YEAR OR SO BEFORE THE MATTER CAME UP, IT WASN'T HOW I THOUGHT OF HER EITHER. I THOUGHT OF HER AS MY FRIEND AND AS

Mo Van the artist. After all, she had a successful art gallery, which is where I met her, on Coast Highway, across the street from the Laguna Art Museum. Her work had been shown in a number of Southern California art shows. So this posing for Playboy thing was just a lark, something to have fun with, something to prove to her grown daughters that she meant it when she said getting older was nothing to worry about. I hadn't seen Mo Van for a year. And then, out of the blue, she called me last Saturday and suggested we get together. "I've got breast cancer," she told me when I asked how she was. She said it almost as casually as she'd once told me she'd posed in Playboy. So we had brunch together the next day at Madison Square & Garden, which is this funky upscale Laguna gift shop and garden café that sprang up in an old house next door to an older, but similar eatery, the Cottage. While the Cottage is a bit hectic and crowded most of the time, Madison Square is more like a restaurant haiku.

Lavender sea static waves like Rose Festival princesses from the river rock garden planters are in front. On the big wooden porch are Chinese nesting boxes and elephant wood carvings. Just inside the front door is a painted bathtub full of rosemary lotions, cherry tomato soaps and Celtic sea slats. It's all very orderly and calming, which, I think, is why Mo Van chose to come here.

Here's the thing about Mo Van. Everybody loves her. I have never been anywhere with her and not had people come over and greet her, give her a hug, ask how she is—men and women. And this was way before cancer made an appearance in her life.

Things are no different this Sunday morning. As

I STAND IN LINE WAITING TO ORDER OUR EGGS AND GERMAN APPLE PANCAKES FROM THE COUNTER, IT SEEMS HALF THE RESTAURANT MILLS ABOUT TO SAY, "HELLO." THERE'S THE YOUNG CLERK WHO HAD CAREFULLY BEEN ARRANGING FRENCH SOAPS ON A COUNTER AND AN OLDER WOMAN IN A FLOWING CHIFFON DRESS WITH PAINT STAINS ON HER HANDS—ANOTHER ARTIST PERHAPS? SHE KISSES MO VAN'S CHEEKS. EVEN THE CAFÉ OWNER, JON MADISON, COMES OUT OF THE KITCHEN TO GIVE MO VAN A HUG WHEN HE SEES HER. HUGS, I THINK, ARE A BIG PART OF HER KARMA. "I'M GLAD YOU'VE COME THIS MORNING," HE SAYS, AND SEEING THE LOOK IN HIS EYE, THE WAY HE TOUCHES HER ARM, YOU HAVE TO BELIEVE HE MEANS IT.

"IS THERE ANYBODY IN LAGUNA YOU DON'T KNOW?" I ASK MO VAN AS WE WALK OUT INTO THE SUNNY GARDEN CARRYING OUR COFFEE AND LOOKING FOR A TABLE.

SHE SMILES, "PROBABLY."

WE SIT BENEATH AN OLD CHINESE ELM IN A GARDEN FILLED WITH POTTED CITRUS TREES AND SCENTED VINES, TALKING ABOUT LIFE. I DON'T WANT TO GET TOO WEIRD HERE, BUT I'M ALMOST CERTAIN MO VAN IS AN AVATAR, WHICH, IF YOU DON'T ALREADY KNOW, IS LIKE A GODDESS WHO GETS BORED UP IN THE HEAVENS AND DECIDES TO COME DOWN TO EARTH IN SOME SORT OF A HUMAN OR ANIMAL INCARNATION. I AM CONVINCED OF THIS BECAUSE MO VAN ALWAYS TELLS ME STARTLING THINGS ABOUT MY LIFE SHE SHOULDN'T KNOW. SOMETIMES IT'S THINGS EVEN I DON'T KNOW, AS IF SHE WERE PRIVY TO INFORMATION THAT I WILL LEARN IN ANOTHER SIX OR NINE MONTHS, IF I'M LUCKY. ONCE I TOLD HER I WAS NO LONGER GOING TO SEE A CERTAIN INDIVIDUAL, SOMEONE SHE'D HEARD ME TALK ABOUT BUT HAD NEVER MET. SHE TOOK ME BY THE ARM AND TOLD ME THAT I WAS WASTING MY TIME. "OF COURSE, YOU'LL SEE HER. IT'S DESTINED. WHY DON'T YOU JUST GET ON WITH IT?" SHE WAS RIGHT, BUT IT TOOK ME ALMOST A YEAR TO FIGURE IT OUT.

This morning, as we sit in Madison's garden, where the air smells of orange blossoms and the sea, she tells me of another reincarnation—her own. "I feel like I am giving birth to myself," she says, fingering the long scarf that covers her head. "I am bald, like a baby, and I'm nauseous in the morning, like when I was pregnant with all my children. And the whole process—from when I learned about the tumor to when I will have completed treatment—is nine months."

She leans across the table and takes my hand. "Something in me is dying," she says, "but it doesn't scare me, because something else, a new me, is being reborn." Then Mo Van, who never likes to spend too much time talking about herself, asks, "What's happening with you?"

"It's a very long story, one that could take all day." I give her the nickel version. She listens intently. When I am done, she is silent for a few minutes though her eyes dance as she stares into my face, as if she were reading my palm.

"It's the same," she says. "Your dilemma and my cancer. They come from the same source. They have just manifested themselves in different ways. You, too, are changing. You, too, are being reborn. Don't be afraid of this, David."

We leave the restaurant arm in arm, crossing to the other side of the street to her gallery. I kiss her good-bye on the cheek and tell her I think she looks quite beautiful, and I mean it. She smiles and pats my arm. As I walk away from her, I feel, for the first time in months, as light as air. I feel as if I am a balloon being carried by the wind high into the sky, away from all the troubles of the earth.

I appreciated the newspaper piece because I hope it would inspire others to keep on pursuing their dreams, no matter what. However, I cherish even more a letter that a visitor, a young, inspiring artist, gave me. He didn't know about the cancer. He just thought I was tired and perhaps thinking of painting less. He sent me these words:

Hello, Mo Van,

I met you at your gallery the other day. I'm the guy you were sure had never been married. I'm just writing to tell you how impressed I am that you've made a name for yourself. I can tell you are a strong individual—the kind that does not accept less than what makes you happy. Anyway, I'm not writing to patronize you, and I know that I'm not very good at that either. The truth is . . . well, I don't know why . . . why . . . I'm writing you. I do know this. The only thing worth anything, yet the one thing most people take for granted, we, you and me, have already given to each other, a "hello." Having gotten the important stuff out of the way, I'll go on to say a few things about a few things. Did you know that Picasso created some 20,000 art pieces during his lifetime and that even in his last years, he created up to 4 a day? You probably do. Me, I only found that out a few days back when I bought this little art book on Picasso, which, by the way, I just love, and I think I got a great deal on it, since I only paid a little over $9 for it. Nice, huh?

I have to confess one thing to you. I was very surprised, and I would venture to say, maybe even a little shocked, at your comment that as of late you feel that you've exhausted your painting talent and creativity. I know these were not your exact words, but I believe this is in fact what you were trying to say. Or not—I don't know. Why I reacted this way, even if I don't show it, was very simply, as I said earlier, that I am impressed at what you've accomplished. You have your own gallery, and, even in your own words, you've been selling paintings for at least 10 years, as I understand it. So, as I'm there beholding your artwork, thinking and re-thinking, a million reasons why I have chosen the right path for myself, that of being an artist, all of a sudden here comes you, the artist, essentially telling me that you're thinking of quitting. WOW! A bit of a shocker, really. Amazingly, that is exactly what I needed to hear at the moment. I don't know how to explain it very well, but the main thing is that I got it—I am doing exactly what I want, need, and should be doing right now. I am an artist. Do you know what impressed me about Picasso? HE HAD BALLS! Big ones, too! Now, I know you're a woman and intelligent, and yes, this is a sexist thing to say, so I know you will not mind my using such language, 'cause more than likely you use it yourself.

Anyway, as I was saying, Picasso had balls, I mean, here's a guy who at the age of 16 already had mastered the old academic style of painting. I mean the whole thing—perspective drawing, lightings, color schemes, composition—you name it, he could do it, and he could have gone on to have a great career as an academic artist, and what does he do instead? The guy is nuts, like any great master, and simply put all that down, basically saying, I give up all that I know about art and, with that, all that I know about me, and trade it for that I DON'T KNOW. Fucking amazing, really. The guy goes on to struggle with his identity for a while, but, not long after, becomes recognized for what he was, and is—a genius. A fucking genius, with balls!

. You, my dear, strike me as a "Picasso." You, woman, are a "Picasso." I know. Believe me, I know because I, too, am a Picasso. You had the balls to say, "I'm going to paint any fucking way I want to paint and make money at it, too. Thank you."

Whatever you do in the future can only matter to you, because it's your decision. What you have done is what matters to others like me, who haven't yet done. Many times I feel that I don't have much to say or that whatever I have to say, nobody wants to hear, and it's only through writing that I feel the most free to express myself, knowing that after you're done reading, all you have to do is crumple the papers and throw them in the trash, but I won't see that happen, will I? I won't see your reaction to these words, will I? I look forward to seeing more artwork from you, whatever form that takes, either more paintings or a book or any other form you choose.

Bon chance! Jose.

P.S. What should I call you? Mo Van, Mo, Monica or —— ?

* * *

I keep the letter well protected at home because this young man seems to have caught the essence of what I've always tried to do with my art.

I continued without a wig even when asked to do a benefit at Hoag Hospital Celebration of Life Day for survivors of cancer, a day of special meaning.

※　※　※

AND THEY CAME

Every year, Hoag Hospital holds a celebration honoring those who are cancer survivors by letting those in attendance participate in a creative afternoon of painting on canvases that are numbered to direct the painters what colors to put where—a "paint by numbers" design. Because I am free in all that I do, I agreed to host a canvas, although I was sweating, bald from my chemotherapy and tired, and I still had radiation to face. I, too, wanted to celebrate life.

However, I said I didn't want any numbers on the canvas. I wanted the guests to have fun on a canvas design I had started. They agreed, somewhat reluctantly, since my work already had some acclaim. I prepared a canvas with a sky and a path. Then moments before the celebration started, I felt the sweat pouring off my face, my stomach churning nauseously, and suddenly I wasn't sure if I could go on with my promise. My daughter, Kristen, who was there to help me lay out the paints, asked with a startled look in her eyes if I was feeling all right.

Having had my last bout of chemo a few days before, I wasn't sure.

Looking up to the ceiling, as if trying to get a glimpse of heaven, I started asking God to please give me the strength to go through with the promise I had made. With my bald head, glistening from the sweat, my shirt sticking to me, I asked my mama and papa if they could be with me, and help me, "Mama, Papa, you know what this is like. Please, help me." I continued. "Dear God, I know I have done it all, and maybe you just wanted me to do cancer, too, just so I would know what it's like. I know now." As I was looking up, I saw a little girl getting on a boat, her sister dying, and her, working, cleaning restaurants, singing, having babies, flying in private jets, sitting and talking with Clint Eastwood, sitting next to Barbara Marx at a Sinatra concert, doing the Phil Donahue show, Leeza, dancing in the streets of San Francisco, posing for Playboy, being beaten in a New York alley, begging God to not let me die there, doing the Breast Cancer Survivors' Parade (I always thought it would be the Rose Bowl parade). My life was passing quickly before my eyes.

"Mom?" Kristen brought me back to the moment. I looked at her and over my painting. An elderly couple stood in front of the canvas. The celebration had begun. I felt like I did when I ran the L.A. Marathon for the first time, with two more miles to go. The silver-haired lady asked, "What do we do here?"

I answered warmly, "You just pick up a brush and paint."

"But there are no numbers." She looked up at the

path, the trees and blue sky I had outlined in light acrylic. She carefully added a few branches to the tree and smiled at me, "I'm an eight-year survivor." She spoke with a heavy accent. Eight. Mama was born on the eighth. A sign; they were with me. I relaxed. I read the lady's name tag, "Henny," and asked her full name.

"You have to guess," the tall, gray-haired gentleman declared.

"Henrietta?"

"No, it's Hendrica." It was the female version of my father's name. More symbols. I asked where they were from.

"Holland," he said. "I was born in Haarlem, and she was born in Castricum." Kristen listened and understood. My papa was born in Haarlem, and Castricum was my mama's hometown and mine. Papa had once told me I would see him in many things. He loved birds, and whenever a bird is near, I think of him. And now this elderly couple. I felt a wave of peace. My daughter wiped my tears. Then the man came back alone, picked up a brush and painted a bird on my canvas. It was a bird like a child would paint, like the letter "M" in the trees.

❀ ❀ ❀

As I awoke in the middle of the night alone, the thought that someone might have painted over my birds startled me. Then I heard the words, "You may not always see me, but I am always there."

That painting, *The Path*, with the bird still there, now hangs in the waiting area in the Cancer Ward at Hoag

Hospital. It is there to honor my parents and all who have had to endure the cancer experience.

* * *

I wanted to honor my family by doing what they couldn't, return to our country. Despite feeling weak and nauseous at times, I felt it was important to make the connection.

Castricum is a small village. When I left there were 11,000 people, and when I returned about 45,000. We left a family of six, and now there were three, my brother and sister and I.

My cousins welcomed me, and we rode bikes around the familiar streets, stopping on Konigin Juliana Str. I walked up the path to my old front door. I wanted to knock and just peek in, but I didn't. The memories of the way it looked before would stay intact. As I walked back to my bike, I imagined retracing my steps to the waiting VW van the day we left for the ship in Rotterdam. Looking at the neighbor's houses, I could see them again. They were standing, waving good-bye to us. I said a silent good-bye to them and went on with my cousin to the old house of my Oma and Opa (grandparents). There, I looked in the window. I could see through the years, grandparents, aunts and uncles, parents, talking, often gathering after church for coffee and pastries. Sometimes Ome Jerry (Uncle Jerry) would visit from America and all the cousins would gather around him and listen to his tales about the "land of opportunity." Often I wondered, *Had he not been such a great storyteller, would my father have made that big, life-changing decision?* None of them were alive now. I started crying uncontrollably. My cousin said nothing. His presence was enough.

I went on to the old church where I used to sit next to my mama, fourth row from the front, but the door was locked during the week to prevent vandalism. There were only enough parishioners now for two Masses a week. It seemed odd that I, having been divorced, was the only one who still attended Mass **regularly**. Maybe I was the one who needed it most.

A lighter note was an eightieth birthday party for one of my aunts. There were cousins I hadn't seen in over thirty years. One surprised me by saying in Dutch, "Your mama was always my favorite aunt. She was the 'coolest' of the sisters, ahead of her time." **My mother**. I tried to picture her in that light, thanking my cousin for the gift.

Later I rode by my old school, remembering how I used to look out that window, daydreaming about orange lemonade. This was the school I dreamed about when I sat in a different classroom, not knowing the language, wishing I were back here. This school's window looked out to the pond where we skated on cold days.

It was also the place where Mr. van Westen punished me by making me stand in the hallway for cutting off my ponytail. He had threatened me more than once that should I ever come to school with short hair, he wouldn't allow me back into the classroom. He kept his promise. Looking at the window of my fifth-grade classroom, I realized that Mr. van Westen might have been my first crush. So many people and places, smells and tastes came rushing back. It was a bittersweet visit, but I'll always be glad I went.

As much as I love Holland, when I returned to LAX, I felt like kissing the ground. This was also where I shared life with my parents, and where my children were born, art discovered me, and I had my friends. It took going back for me to realize America was truly my home. I realized how much my parents had sacrificed to bring us here in hopes of finding a better life. And when I touched the ground, still facing radiation and the uncertainty of my health, I silently thanked my parents for all the things I had taken for granted. And someone else was glad we had made that long journey so many years ago.

Hi Mom,

I'm glad Nanny, Papa, you and the rest of your family were brave and came to America on that boat so you could become my mother. I'm glad that you met Dad and had us all. You have such courage in taking care of us. I hope I can be that way when I am a mother. Having worked with you for so many years, I see the way people react when you are near, the way you make them feel, not just us. I am so glad you and Dad have always remained friends, never making us children aware of your differences. If there is one thing in my life I am absolutely sure, 100% sure, of, it is that you truly love us, as all of us do you.

Love, Andrea, the hand.

X.

The Trinity:
Three Wise Men

Springtime in Avignon

Once you've experienced any trauma, such as abuse, war, or illness, there are others who can benefit from the experience, telling their tales, too, or just gaining courage from yours. In California, sometimes the only time neighbors talk is just after an earthquake. The need to validate the event overcomes any reserve. I found this need to share to be a benefit of having experienced the word that was barely mentioned a few generations ago.

Now, I who had changed channels when cancer was mentioned, avoiding it in magazines, was able to talk about it. I joined in the Susan B. Komen 5K Race for the Cure, with friends, family, survivors all running together. I also walked in the Breast Cancer Survivors parade. My children and grandchildren were on the sidelines cheering me on. As I marched in my pink cap and pink t-shirt, I yelled to them, "I always thought it would be the Rose Parade." Both the race and parade are important to raise awareness and encourage women to be tested, but I didn't enjoy the parade. I didn't like people looking at us as heroes, when all we'd done was have a disease and survive, but the sheer visual number of marchers each year proves that the disease can be beaten.

Before my diagnosis, three men had come into my gallery. The galleries next to me had previously received a visit from Mick Jagger, but my guests turned out to be far more special. The three came in and quietly looked around. In a town like Laguna, I was used to seeing men traveling together. I waited and watched. One went to look at the far wall, one the south wall, and one stayed in the main studio, which is west. Without realizing it, they formed a cross with their positions. Strange. Then one spoke, "Hi, I'm Chris. Who's the artist?"

I answered with my usual, "If you like the work, it's me. If not, he's not here."

He laughed. "I like it." We talked art, and he introduced the others as John and Brian. He said he was an art therapist, so we talked of the healing powers of art. Later, he reintroduced them as actually being Father Chris and Father Jude and Brother Brian. I knew my mother must be smiling to know I was surrounded by three priests, and not the "Tom, Dick, and Harry" she thought I'd be with when she learned of my divorce. I told them I was Catholic, but I wasn't sure the church still claimed me, as I had been divorced.

They didn't seem to care and continued talking with me, making me feel important, becoming my friends. I later told my daughters that the other gallery could have Mick Jagger, I had my holy men.

It was even more a blessing when soon after I was faced with the news of cancer, and I called Father Chris to have someone in whom to confide. His warm voice quickly crossed the miles from Chicago to California and gave me courage. "You've called the right person. I'm the national director of the St. Peregrine Ministries. He's the patron saint of those with cancer."

How did it happen that just before I was to hear my dreadful news, I had met the man who gave comfort to those who have cancer? It certainly seemed a divine intervention. I poured out my story, including that my sister, mother, father, and uncle had passed on due to cancer. He was a compassionate listener.

Later, the three men came to California and invited me out to eat on the San Clemente pier. It was a great place with a spectacular view. I had been there years before with my brother and my children. I'd asked my brother, "Do you believe in heaven?"

He'd given a surprised look, but answered immediately, "Yeah, why?"

"Because if there is a heaven, I've just had a glimpse of it here." The sun had been shining bright, it was an unusually warm day, and when we reached the end of the pier, I was in alignment with the sun, and for a moment I had a glimpse of heaven. A oneness with everything good in life, being with my children, my brother, and the beauty all around. It was a perfect moment in time I cherished.

Now, I was there with two priests and a brother. I was dining with the Trinity. Father Jude took me outside and declared, "If you even think of paying for any of this, I'll break your arms." He looked like he could do it, if he ever wanted. I agreed to accept their hospitality. They told me about St. Peregrine who was a member of the Order of Friars Servants of Mary in the 1300s. He had a sore, which we think now must have been cancer. He prayed all night before they were going to cut off his leg, and in the morning, the sore was gone. He continued to help the sick. Today, around the world, people pray to him and celebrate his day on the 5th of November.

I helped Father Chris with correspondence to others with cancer, a story in the newspaper and as a supporter of their work. I speak to others to share, listen and give them courage. I certainly had and have so much to be thankful for. I thank God for allowing me to share my art. I had faced cancer head-on. I realize now that I don't need to fear anything anymore. I've looked at the thought of death, and I am alive. I am very alive each and every day. What I didn't know then was that love was just around the corner, arriving when I least expected.

❊ ❊ ❊

After some negative experiences with priests, these three restored my faith in who a man of the cloth could be. They respected my life and inspired me with theirs. They're strengthened by faith.

FAITH

IT DOESN'T MATTER HOW FAMOUS YOU ARE, NO ONE CARES IN HEAVEN.

❊ ❊ ❊

THE WORSE KIND OF HELL WOULD BE TO HAVE KNOWN WHAT HEAVEN WAS LIKE.

❊ ❊ ❊

XI.

Take Three:
A Gift of Love

Out of a Window

When I was first diagnosed with breast cancer, my outlook completely changed. I was still cheerful and happy to be alive. Even though sweaty, bald and often nauseous, I kept the playful spirit for which I was known. Without the continued support of my children and friends, however, the struggle to keep a positive attitude would have been much more difficult. Family and friends are the flowers of our gardens, and we are, of theirs. I was content. The last thing on my mind was meeting a man.

Along with my family, the one constant was my faith. I spent many hours in church praying. If God deemed that I was to meet someone, he had to be someone with whom I could share my faith. I had lived long enough and experienced enough to know I would always have my trust in and love of God. This love had never gotten old or tiring. I had known sex, money, recognition, and admiration for my exterior and inner selves—all these were temporary.

No matter how terrible I felt, I managed to sit attentively through Mass, wiping my forehead, face, and neck with tissues and paper towels. My chemotherapy had deprived me of my hair, but not my faith.

One Sunday after Mass, a handsome and dignified man approached me. He had slightly unruly gray hair, a shirt almost tucked into his jeans, and wore sandals.

"Are you MoVan, the artist?" he asked. "I'm Bill Lee."

"Yes, I'm Movan. Wait, are you the mystery commission?"

"Guilty," he smiled.

Weeks before, I had received an e-mail from someone requesting a painting of the Blessed Mother in a garden setting. Not knowing who wanted to commission me, I had asked for more information. Now I was looking at the face of the requester.

"Well, it's very nice to meet you." I extended my hand, realizing at the last second it held my damp paper towel. Quickly shoving it in my pocket, I blushed as I reoffered my hand. His face looked nicely familiar.

"We have a friend in common," he said. "Jim, your sometimes limousine driver from Dana Point."

"Yes. I've known Jim for several years. Actually, he attends this church."

"Indeed." Bill paused as if he had more to say. "I brought you something. I've been watching you for weeks and . . ." He hesitated and reached into his sport coat pocket and pulled out a box with fifty cotton handkerchiefs.

"What's this?" I asked, puzzled.

As he put the box in my hand, he looked right into my eyes. "I never want to see a paper towel touch your face again." Had I a full head of perfectly braided hair, I could not have felt more beautiful. God was indeed moving in His mysterious way. We made plans to see each other again. I was truly taken by this man, who was not only kind and thoughtful but wasn't intimidated by a bald lady going through chemotherapy. Our courtship began slowly—having lunch and attending church. We were both people of faith, and we were each thrilled to find that the other felt just as connected to God.

Besides lunches and church, there was the modern courtship—e-mail. Bill cheered me up and gave me an insight into his thoughts and feelings with letters:

✽ ✽ ✽

Monica,

Our friend, Jim, asked me what I thought of you. I told him I thought you were the most beautiful woman I had ever met, inside and out.

And you asked me a great question today that I didn't answer, "What do you see yourself doing when you are sixty-five?" I thought about it later. Here are my quick thoughts:

Going to daily Mass, living within walking distance from the beach, surfing (at least boogie boarding), walking, kayaking, listening to great music, traveling to new places, learning local customs and culture, growing flowers and fruits, hanging out in bookstores, doing real estate deals once or twice a year as an investor, speaking to my children most days, babysitting my grandchildren, and sharing all of the above with a woman who enjoys much of it (not all, except Mass), who has a sense of self that is not threatened by my interests such that she can enjoy her own at any time and is anxious to include me whenever possible, loves life, is always questioning and learning, loves to touch and be touched. I will tell her every day how beautiful she is and how lucky I feel being with her, not because she needs to hear it, but because I need to say it.

Hopefully, that doesn't sound selfish, and . . . the lady exists. You make me smile. If you're back early, I'll pull into Dietrich's at 9:15 for coffee.

❀   ❀   ❀

I was there at 9:15, too.

❀   ❀   ❀

So that was Bill, a man whose company I enjoyed. But all I really knew was that he liked gardening, going to daily

Mass, basketball, the Anaheim Angels, movies, and that he was in the process of getting a divorce. I liked him and what I read in his e-mails to me, but he didn't mention dancing. How did he feel about this passion of mine? Certainly not wanting to mislead him, after several weeks of lunches, e-mail, and liturgies, I suggested he visit me at home. Once there, I announced, "Bill, there is another side of me besides the Catholic cancer patient." Handing him a glass of wine, I settled next to him on the couch and waited.

"Really?" was all the said.

I prepared myself to confess. "I love to dance, sing, and have fun." I half expected him to pop up and make his excuses on his way out. He had seemed rather serious.

Instead, I heard, "So do I." My heart did a back flip in my chest.

Without a word, I got up from the couch, walked to the stereo and carefully selected a CD. The slow notes of Barry White's "Oh, What A Night for Dancing" filled the room, and I began to waltz around, closing my eyes to soak up the sounds, as I was used to doing when I danced alone, only this time, with the extra delight of just knowing Bill was there. I was unaware that he had put down his glass until I felt his cool hand on the small of my back. He pulled me closer, and we danced.

※　※　※

He was my comfort, and I his. In his soft sweaters and sandals, this man who was equally at home on a surfboard or an office, was so at peace. He accompanied me to my visits to the oncologist, holding my hand, asking questions and listening intently.

We met at church, and that continued and continues to be part of our beings. Unfortunately we ran into some of the same types of priests and judging parishioners I had met alone.

At first when we went to church, we each went alone. Later, we went together. Those who had known my husband, short of shunning him and me, were busy judging what they did not know. Some looked at us with a holier-than-thou attitude. Yet many of these same people had no trouble with the fact that the monsignor, to whom we had gone for counsel, was the primary reason the Catholic Church had to pay out its biggest settlement to date, for his having been again accused of *improper behavior with young men while he was the principal of an all-Catholic high school.* * * * *

Forgive me, Father, for I have sinned.

The old priest stood at the door. He had been there a long time. I commented on his Irish sweater he wore on St. Patrick's Day. He nodded, but without a smile. Again, I felt that feeling in my stomach, that maybe I was not welcome here at my old church. I looked at Bill and asked, "Is it just my imagination, or was the Father just an old grump?" The Irish, burly-looking priest sure wasn't doing much uplifting of spirits, standing there at the entrance looking like he hadn't done his daily duty yet. I started to wonder what we were doing in this church. And when I extended my hand to a fellow parishioner in welcome with "Peace be with you," the woman whom I had known and taken a Bible class with looked at me with disdain. *It wasn't but a month or two before the priest in the sweater was removed quietly and,*

151

again, his name appeared in the paper for not knowing
boundaries with children many years prior.
Forgive me, Father, for I have sinned.
But there were others, positive others.

Once when Bill and I were at church, they had a general absolution Mass. Many priests came to hear confessions, and were positioned around the church. Bill and I went around the corner to one. I went first. Before I could speak, he said to me in a kind voice, "I forgive you, my child." I wanted to kiss him for that. He didn't need to hear what my confession was. My simple presence there, my wanting to confess was enough. He had the compassion people go to church to receive.

* * *

Later we were at a Catholic retreat. A priest who was speaking gave his opinion of communion: "I believe everyone who shows up in church should be served communion. They come to church to be closer to Christ. Who are we to judge?" His words were a welcome change.

* * *

So, since we were there, as I had once been, to be near God, we continued to go. Our love *was blossoming*, and we thanked God, as we moved toward uniting this love.

* * *

Even as a child, I never fantasized about my wedding as some girls do, but my wedding to Bill on the surf in Maui was the stuff of which dreams are made. We returned to our favorite vacation spot with my daughter Laura, her husband,

Paulo, and my fourteen-year-old grandson, also Paulo. We spent the day laughing, swimming, and enjoying the sunshine. At three in the afternoon, we returned to our cottage to dress. That's when I found, true to our family custom, the letter from Laura.

Dear Mom, Movan, Monica Lee—

Mommy, best wishes on your wedding day. You are like a song for all of us. It never gets old; it just makes us happy every time we hear it. We want to sing along. A good song can touch you in a certain way and make your day better. You have a light inside that shines so brightly for all of us, children, grandchildren, and now, for Bill.

I believe we are all given certain gifts in life. You are one of mine.

Be happy, the two of you, for always.

Love, LAURA

(Your firstborn daughter)

❀ ❀ ❀

And then we were outside by the beach, Bill and I. He was dashing, as always, in a black collared shirt and crisp beige linen slacks. I felt like a teenager again in a flowing white skirt and peasant top. Hand in hand we returned to the spot where we had been frolicking in the waves just an hour before. The twinkling sounds of the harp underscored our ceremony, and there, in the golden light, foam tickling our toes, a simple gold band was slipped on my finger.

* * *

When Bill looks at me, I know he thinks I am beautiful. When he listens intently and doesn't interrupt my wild ramblings, I know he thinks I'm smart. If I sing off-key on meandering Sunday drives, he looks at me, and though I'm sure he'd rather listen to the radio, he smiles. When I take off my clothes, he looks at my body, and I know he thinks my breasts are beautiful, even though they're scarred from surgery.

In my dances with others, I learned, above all, that love is not enough. I love so many things, people, nature, and music. However, though I have been close to many men, I knew I could not be married to them. I loved an artist for the way he made a canvas come alive. I loved a funny man who could do impersonations like no other. I loved a man who sang off-key, but sang anyway. I loved a man for making me music tapes to play whenever I felt lonely. I also loved a man for the way he said my name, with his Polish accent.

But ultimately, in Bill, I have found the partner I was seeking. . .or was it that I had found myself? Literally and figuratively. It is his soul I feel connected to. Our movements are so well choreographed that we no longer know who is leading, and who is following. And I must say, the choreographer did a much better job this time than the time we ran into each other at Birmingham High School when he told me to never "stop smiling like that." And when he repeated those very same words shortly after he left my gallery the first time, something vaguely familiar reminded me of another man, another time but had not connected him yet. His casual dress should have alerted me, his shirt still almost tucked in, and the sandals still the same, with that unruly, once-blonde-now-almost-champagne white hair tousled as if he just jumped out of bed.

It was he who coached the children's basketball team at our Lady of Lourdes, in the San Fernando Valley, when my son was in first grade, and too young to be on the team. I had had a glimpse of him then, not knowing I had run into him a few years before. He had been the surfer my friend Lara had told me about so many years ago, a surfer with three boys. The man whom I had given thought to, on my infrequent returns to Dana Point, and unconsciously wondered if he and Lara ever ended up together. He, the man who cannot keep his shirts tucked in, is still telling me to "always keep smiling like that," forty-two years later. The music of mutual respect and understanding carries us into the world and brings us back together in synchronicity.

※　※　※

Marriage is more than a rite of passage into adulthood. It's a dance of precision and grace that not everyone is ready to perform. Before you jump head first into the pool, you must trust your partner and know that it's okay to come up for air. Our culture puts such an importance on a **conventional way of behavior** that is rarely understood or truly appreciated. I believe that before you can swim on a team, you have to learn to swim on your own, and I did.

※ ※ ※

Being comfortable anywhere, Bill and I feel at home walking on the pier in Santa Monica or going into an elite restaurant as I did once, when we were driving at night, wearing pajamas. As much as it is possible in life, I believe you should be with whom you want, where you want, and just be you.

I remember:

We were coming back from Orange County on a Sunday night, and we stopped at the upscale Biltmore Hotel and Restaurant. Bill likes their hamburgers, and I their soup. Since I was driving, I had changed into my more comfortable grey-and-white gingham pajama bottoms. Above I was wearing my silk black-and-white blouse and a black silk scarf. Bill looked at me. Yes, I was going in that way. I tucked my pajamas into my Ugg boots, put on a jacket, and walked unabashedly in, despite the fact that everyone else was formally dressed. They not only seated us, but in a wonderful corner where they seat notables. Bill and I were laughing so hard, but I was just being me. Then, of course, I had to go to the bathroom. He cringed a little, "I know you're not going to walk through this dining room like that." So, naturally, I did. It was great. Bill was so proud. From the waist up I was Grace Kelly, from the waist down Hobo Kelly, but I was myself.

※ ※ ※

One Christmas season, we were in Santa Monica on the Venice Pier Boardwalk. There were street artists, singers, musicians, and dancers. The whole place was alive. Then we went to Rodeo Drive, an elite street in Beverly Hills, the shopping mecca, with imported French and Italian fashions and exquisite jewelers. We had read that it was going to be lit up, and it was. There were elaborate Christmas decorations including a much-written-about multi-million-dollar chandelier. But it was all so tastefully correct and sterile. We saw only a few people gazing through windows, but no one shopping. There was no atmosphere, no creativity of singing or dancing people in the street. We went back to Venice where there was life, excitement, and hope in the eyes of the people showing their wares. It felt like Christmas.

This is us. This is love. Whenever, wherever it comes, embrace it.

I believe in Life, Love, and Marriage.

LIFE

BEING YOUNG AND BEAUTIFUL IS A "GIMME."
BEING OLD AND BEAUTIFUL IS AN ACCOMPLISHMENT.

❀   ❀   ❀

IT IS HARD TO KEEP ONE'S OPINIONS TO ONESELF.

❀   ❀   ❀

IT IS DIFFICULT TO LOVE EVERYONE.

❀   ❀   ❀

IT TAKES MORE GUTS TO APOLOGIZE, THAN TO ACCEPT AN APOLOGY.

❀   ❀   ❀

MOST COMEDIANS ARE NOT FUNNY IN REAL LIFE.

❀ ❀ ❀

AS YOUNG OR BEAUTIFUL AS ONE IS, THERE WILL ALWAYS BE
SOMEONE YOUNGER AND MORE BEAUTIFUL NOT FAR BEHIND.

❀ ❀ ❀

LOVE

YOU CAN SEND A MAN ALL THE CARDS, LOVE LETTERS, OR GIFTS;
IT IS NOT GOING TO MAKE HIM LOVE YOU, AND VICE-VERSA.

❀ ❀ ❀

MARRIAGE

NO ONE CAN BREAK UP A MARRIAGE.

❀ ❀ ❀

THERE IS NOTHING BETTER THAN A "GOOD MARRIAGE" AND
NOTHING WORSE THAN A BAD ONE.

❀ ❀ ❀

HAVING BEEN MARRIED MORE THAN ONCE DOESN'T MEAN WE
FAILED; IT JUST MEANS WE KEPT TRYING TO GET IT RIGHT, BUT NOT
AT THE EXPENSE OF MAKING OTHERS MISERABLE.

❀ ❀ ❀

IT'S BETTER TO COME FROM A BROKEN HOME THAN TO LIVE IN
ONE.

❀ ❀ ❀

XII.

Because You Can

Hotel De Europe

I'm still here. It took me well over a year to put these words down on paper. I never claimed to be a writer, just had the will to do so. I am the woman who paints, dances, boogie boards in the cold Pacific (with a wet suit from head to toe), cries, laughs and still sings off-key, gardens, believes in miracles and, perhaps to some, I'm just the lady you saw with twelve items in the ten item line. We meet briefly or for a lifetime, in person, on the web, or in the pages of this book.

The truth is, looking back, I wish my first marriage could have been successful, so that I could now say, "I have been married, happily, for almost 40 years." But getting married so young is a mistake. I envy no one, and never have, but there are times when, upon meeting a long-married couple who are enjoying their grandchildren together, I feel that somehow, knowing what I know now, I would have been less selfish by not leaving the father of my children so long ago. We all need to be better prepared for something so life-altering as marriage. How many of us really give thought to how it affects our children when a marriage breaks up? We talk ourselves into believing that "it is best for everyone." I did. I believed it at the time, but had no idea what it meant to be a family affected by divorce. We are as intact as can be, now, with 8 stepbrothers and stepsisters, 7 grandchildren, etc. And there will be 22 around the table at Thanksgiving. There will be love, laughter and sharing. But as a mother looking at her children, I cannot help but wonder what they are thinking. Do they think of what it might have been like had their father been sitting at the head of the table? Do his children look at me and wonder what it would have been like had their mother gotten up early to put the turkey in the oven? We don't know the answers, and we don't have to know.

I will continue to tell my children not to give up as problems arise in their unions. I will tell them "nothing in life is easy." I will admit that I hadn't a clue what I was giving up when I left their father so long ago. I did not know that I would not look at him when our first grandchild entered this world and, in that very moment, realize that one gives up a lot when making a decision that affects so many. I will tell my children and anyone who is willing to listen.

I love my husband. He may not be the father of all the children sitting around the Thanksgiving table, but he is the man whose hand I hold as we pray together; he is the one I talk to about how unprepared most of us are when we say "I do." He is the one who understands how important family is, as we make no distinction between his, mine or ours. He's the man I am grateful for as we give thanks around the dining room table.

I never worried about making a "perfect picture," as nothing in life is perfect. Do the best we can, 'go for it' without worrying how it might be perceived by others. Love life everyday, keeping our eyes open for the miracles that surround us if only we are willing to see them.

With or without children, we all eventually have to live with ourselves, and that involves waiting, waiting for a friend, waiting for the car to turn in our driveway with children and grandchildren, puppies, and people asking for directions. Always waiting for events or people as I waited with my sisters for our aunt and uncle to drive up and give us a short ride to our home on Koninging Juliana Str. Waiting for the ship to reach America. Waiting to find true love (and it came when I wasn't looking). Waiting for a phone call from the doctor. Waiting to find out about surf conditions so I can take the boogie board out. Waiting again to find out about my latest ultrasound because the doctor found a suspicious little lump in my other breast. Now I wait to see what each day will bring. When the sun comes up we are given a brand new twenty-four hours to discover new things, repeat the old, enjoy those around us, do some little kindness and be better than we were the day before.

I NEVER KNEW HOW TO WRITE A BOOK, AND NOW I HAVE.

SURF'S UP, SO I THINK I'LL GRAB MY BOOGIE BOARD AND CATCH A FEW WAVES WITH MY GRANDSON.

M.V.L

About the Author

The author lives on the Central Coast of California between Los Angeles and San Francisco, with her husband Bill and their cat Cosmo. They enjoy frequent visits from deer, foxes, egrets, and many other exotic birds at their home; every October, they're hosts to thousands of Monarch Butterflies who seek refuge on their property as they journey southward.

Mo Van (57) and her husband Bill (63) are often seen boogie boarding between Huntington Beach, where they own a small cottage, and Morro Bay—regardless of the time of year. Mo Van still paints almost daily; she also walks the beaches in search of special driftwood, shells, and other items indigenous to the area. Mo Van and Bill have 8 children between them.

She does yoga regularly and is looking forward to holding retreats at her ranch for women who wish to express themselves through art, yoga, meditation, or music, or who just have a need to 'unwind' and 'regroup.' Her aim is for women to embrace who they are and all the possibilities that lie within them.